FORM AND EVENT

FORDHAM UNIVERSITY PRESS   NEW YORK 2020

COMMONALITIES
Timothy C. Campbell, series editor

FORM AND EVENT

*Principles for an Interpretation
of the Greek World*

CARLO DIANO

Translated by Timothy C. Campbell and Lia Turtas
Introduction by Jacques Lezra

Form and Event was originally published in Italian as *Forma ed evento. Principi per una interpretazione del mondo greco* by Neri Pozza Editore in 1952, 1960, and 1967, and in a fourth edition by Marsilio Editori in 1993.

The translation of this work has been funded by SEPS.

SEPS - Segretariato Europeo per le Pubblicazioni Scientifiche
Via Val d'Aposa 7 - 40123 Bologna - Italy
T. +39 051 271992 - F. +39 051 265983
www.seps.it

Visit us online at www.fordhampress.com.

Library of Congress Cataloging-in-Publication Data available online at https://catalog.loc.gov.

Printed in the United States of America

22 21 20 5 4 3 2 1

First edition

CONTENTS

FORM AND EVENT

INTRODUCTION

JACQUES LEZRA

> The king cannot engage in dialectics with the court jester, or vice versa.
>
> —CARLO DIANO, *FORM AND EVENT*

> Do people understand the nature of the task I dared to stir up with this book?
>
> —FRIEDRICH NIETZSCHE,
> "ATTEMPT AT SELF-CRITICISM" (1886)

Forma ed evento. Principi per una interpretazione del mondo greco, is the decisive work of one of Italy's most distinguished philologists and classical philosophers, and of one of the most original European thinkers of the postwar period. Perhaps because the accent has tended to fall on Carlo Diano's scholarship in classical philology rather than in philosophy, his body of work, while recognized by specialists inside and outside the Italian and to some degree the European academic context, is scarcely known more broadly, especially in the English-speaking world. A distinguished translator, editor, and commentator of the works of Epicurus, of Plato, Aristotle, Menander, Solon, Heraclitus, and the corpus of Greek tragedy (*Il teatro greco: Tutte le tragedie*, 1970, with an important introduction, "L'evento nella tragedia attica"), Diano is author also of *Notes for a Phenomenology of Art* (1954), *Saggezza e poetiche degli antichi* (1968), *Studi e saggi di filosofia antica* (1973), *Scritti epicurei* (1974), and two collections of poems, *L'acqua del tempo* (1933) and the posthumous *Il limite azzurro* (1976). *Forma ed evento*—first published as a long essay in 1952 in the *Giornale critico della filosofia italiana*, then republished that year in book form; then again in 1960 with (as an appendix) a letter, "Forma ed evento," to Pietro de Francisci (responding to de Francisci's critique of the 1952 *Forma ed evento*); in 1967; and in 1993—is Diano's most systematic articulation of a "theoretical tension" (as Remo Bodei puts it in his introduction to the 1994 edition[1]) constitutive not just of the "Greek world," but also of the languages developed to interpret, to translate, and to displace that constitutive tension. To say "languages," though, may be to give too partial a sense of Diano's project in the pages that follow. What the European tradition has called "philosophy," indeed what that tradition is used to calling "Europe" and "tradition" themselves, take shape as responses—denegations, evasions, rearticulations, attempted solutions to or compromises with—that tension.

Form and Event provides not just "principles for an interpretation" of that imaginary object, thing or group of things, practices, conventions and uses called roughly "il mondo greco," but also the principles for mapping, interpreting, and perhaps striking off from the historical paths that "world" takes in forming the principles of Western Europe's fantasy of and claims to cultural hegemony. This second project, in appearance parasitical upon the more restricted philological one, in fact is Diano's first concern—as it should be of first concern today, a moment marked by the tensions between incompatible forms of cosmopolitanism (political, social), the violences that attend the unequal globalization of capital, and the terror of the accelerating, oncoming-occurring event of environmental catastrophe. The philosophically crucial lever of Diano's project? The weakening or loosening of the logical-cultural notions of necessity and singularity.

Today the philosophy of the event, for much of the twentieth century the preserve of phenomenology and phenomenological ontology (think of Heidegger's treatment of *Ereignis*, event, propriative event, "enowing," already in *Being and Time* but especially as of the 1936 *Beiträge*), has been recast in Alain Badiou's searching and controversial treatment of its subtractive mathematical ontology; form and formalisms are a matter of

renewed discussion in the United States and Britain—
not only with the emergence in poetic practice and in
legal thought in the United States of so-called "new"
formalisms in the 1990s, but also in more recent and
conceptually attentive works like Tom Eyers's *Speculative Formalism: Literature, Theory, and the Critical
Present*, Caroline Levine's *Forms: Whole, Rhythm, Hierarchy, Network* or Anna Kornbluh's *The Order of Forms*.
Today, historiography (after Foucault; after the anti-
foundationalist turn in philosophy and in social sciences; after the mid-century crisis of so-called evental
historiography, the rise of *histoire non-événementielle*,
and then what Paul Ricoeur memorably called, in 1992,
"the return of the event") concerns itself with the historicity of positive "facts" or of the concept of "fact" itself
(see Mary Poovey's work), or seeks to sketch what Ethan
Kleinberg calls "a deconstructive approach to the past."
Today Diano's tense interpretation of the *forma-evento*
couple is indispensable.[2]

It will not do, however, to look to Diano's essay just
for genealogies of the terms' uses alone or in relation to
each other. These are provided, but the project of a philological genealogy is not the most pressing. Other cou-
ples, couplets, or triplets have served others to interpret
the "Greek world," and these couplets and triplets and
their destinies color Diano's. Proper names and common; Greek terms, French, German. German Helleno-
philia is a well-known, indeed excessively stressed
phenomenon, but the gesture of organizing the "Greek

world" and the history of that gesture's consequences are broader. Apollo and Dionysus, "myth" and "tragedy" in Jean-Pierre Vernant and Pierre Vidal-Naquet; for Simone Weil, "force" and "the extraordinary sense of equity [*équité*] which breathes through the Iliad."[3] Hans Kelsen: *Geist* and *Seele*. Sigmund Freud: *Eros* and *Ananke*, and *Thanatos*, the death drive. Asymmetrically opposed, the terms in these sets (and more, dropped like magnets into fields of iron filings) are evidence of the different, fantastic, and phantasmatic weights "the Greek world" bears at different moments, for different cultures and academic disciplines, to various effects.[4]

Diano's *Form and Event* is part of the long effort that members of European cultural elites make to legitimate their genealogy invoking a spectral Greek legacy they seek to describe, interpret, and summon. Like the most responsible and original of these, he does not provide a conceptual synthesis of his organizing terms—of form and event (what Diano refers to as "the mystical identity of the principle governing both"). Nor are we dealing here, narrowly, with what the subtitle to *Forma ed evento* offers: "Principles for an interpretation of the Greek world." (A rather condescending early review of *Forma ed evento* remarks that "Diano finds his two categories helpful in taking a synoptic view of ancient civilization."[5]) Something else is at stake, just as something other than "a synoptic view" of antiquity lies behind and before Weil's analysis of the world of the *Iliad*, or Freud's of civilization and its discontents, or that other great project of thinking a classic, irresolvably tense relation and its historical, philological, cultural, and philosophical manifestations and descriptions, Nietzsche's *Birth of Tragedy*.

Just what? In question is precisely what counts or can be made to serve *as* a principle—that is, as a *principium*, a nonanalyzable term that is also though not necessarily compatibly the *beginning* of a series; what counts *as* an axiom of interpretation, conduct, description, judgment, identity—that is, what is in question in *Form and Event* is precisely what counts or can be made to serve as a principle for the conceptual lexicon of European modernity.

Take the subject of Diano's description of what is on offer in his project. An "interpretation," stress on *an, one* interpretation, "una *interpretazione*," is offered to *an* interpretant, we might say (just altering one of Peirce's formulas)—*one* to *one,* a face-off of particulars entailing no general claims. Although the opening to the interpretant is given (it is a *principle*: structural, formal, and abstract), nonetheless and at some time, *if* this or that condition obtains, *if* contingencies prevail, *then* this-or-that interpreter eventually steps into the role-opening, and adapts the "interpretation of the world" to herself and to the circumstances that form the interpretant's "world," in ways we could call dialectical, occasional, pragmatic, and so on. What is the relation between the *formal* principle that commands that "an interpretation" open to an interpretant, and the eventual arrival-on-scene of this-or-that interpreter, where "this-or-that" is the marker of irreducible contingency, hypothesis: of *this* face rather than that? (A clear line of thought links Diano's question to Giorgio Agamben's influential description of the "whatever singularity," *quodlibet* in Latin, *qualunque* in Italian, which will be the principle of what he calls the "coming community.")

And consider the object. "Il mondo greco" is a different thing in 1952 than it was in 1872 or in 1886 (when Nietzsche wrote the "Attempt at Self-Criticism" concerning *The Birth of Tragedy*), and a different thing yet again from what it was when Epicurus laid out the atomic doctrines, or when Lucretius sang them in *De rerum natura* centuries after, and it is different again at each of these times from what it may be today. These differences in the object are, to be sure, in part differences in the *interpretation* of that object, "il mondo greco." But they are more and other than that, not only because an interpretation's interpretant is not, as above, given, but also because what counts as an "object" is not given either: It is not an *idea,* and its coming-on-stage as the first principle of *an* interpretation (the interpretation of *an* object) is only an *event* once an interpretation of that object, "the event," has been agreed or stipulated. The double regression we face, subjective and objective, seems to call for a first baptism of the event, the first event as form-giving: the name that the world was once made to bear for *an* interpretant, "il mondo greco" or "today." With what success and consequences, we will see.

A note first to introduce Carlo Diano.

Born in 1902 in Monteleone di Calabria (now Vibo Valentia), he completed an undergraduate degree at the Sapienza Università di Roma (with a thesis on Leopardi), then taught Latin and Greek language and literature in high schools in Vibo, Viterbo, in Naples (where he briefly was part of the circle of Benedetto Croce), and finally in Rome. In 1933 Diano was seconded by the Mussolini government's Ministry of Foreign Affairs to assume the position of Reader in Italian Literature at the universities of Lund, Copenhagen, and Göteborg. He returned to Italy in 1940 having, among other things, translated into Italian Sven Hedin's 1940 travelogue *The Wandering Lake* (*Il lago errante*, 1941), and in Italy assumed a post in the national Bibliographic Commission (Soprintendenza bibliografica) in Padua.

Despite these appointments, Diano's relation to the Fascist government was hardly transparent. Called on to join the party (as was expected of teachers in the late 1920s) he refused—a decision that could have had grave consequences for his early career. On the other hand, from January 1944 to April 1945 Diano *did* serve as Inspector of Classical Studies for the National Education Ministry of the notorious Repubblica Sociale Italiana (the so-called Republic of Salò).[6] Accepting to hold that position *did* have grave consequences once the war ended. After the fall of the Fascist government, Diano as well as other Paduan philosophers who also held posts in the Repubblica Sociale Italiana were briefly purged from academic appointments. The choice to accept the appointment was consonant with Diano's decision to close his edition of Epicurus's *Ethics* (*Epicuri Ethica*, 1946) with lines warmly recollecting his teacher, Giovanni Gentile, "quem magistrum adulescens audivi, colui deinceps ut patrem, cuius memoria numquam animo excidet meo." Paying homage to Gentile just after the war was a perilous matter. Croce called Gentile, who in 1925 published the *Manifesto degli intellettuali italiani fascisti* and wrote much of the entry on "La dottrina del fascismo" for the 1932 *Enciclopedia Italiana*, "the official philosopher of Fascism in Italy." After the defeat of Fascism in Italy, the memory of Gentile, who was assassinated in 1944, was reviled. Once Diano's period of exclusion ended, he taught at the University of Bari and then, from 1950, at the University of Padua until his death in 1974. Diano was also a painter and a composer, having studied at the Santa Cecilia Conservatory in Rome.

Retain from this short sketch: Diano's illustrious career in the Italian academy was never cloistered; his thought and writing, even his translations from the Swedish, are devoted constantly to discovering principles for the interpretation of the world about him—whether these principles were to be found in the interpretation of a remote Greek world, or in the account furnished by a colonial geographer of the wandering, *errare*, of a remote Chinese lake, as in Hedin's travelogue.

Form and *event* render the Greek terms "idea" (ἰδέα [*idea*], εἶδος [*eidos*]) and "tyche" (τύχη, a word whose sense covers those "accidents" of "fortune" that affect "beings capable of enjoying good fortune, or more generally of 'doing well' or 'doing ill,' in the sense either of 'faring' or of 'acting' so," as Aristotle's commentators P. H. Wicksteed and F. M. Cornford put it; *tyche* is a species of *automaton*, those chance events affecting all natural beings).[7] Diano's essay opens on a "technical" question arising from the difference between the Aristotelian syllogism and the Stoic syllogism, and shows the unresolved difference between the two to be a type of an irresolution that characterizes the broader "mondo greco" and—by implication, by analogy, by extrapolation—the cultures and modes of thought for which that world serves as a principle. "Da un lato il sillogismo categorico della forma che ignora gli eventi, dall'altro il sillogismo ipotetico dell'evento che ignora le forme," he writes: "On one hand, we have the categorical syllogism of the form that pays no mind of events. On the other, we have the hypothetical syllogism of the event that ignores forms." The movement from a "technical" point of logic to the interpretation of a "world" will only be surprising if we set aside the expansive sense that logos has in the context Diano opens on:

notoriously, λόγος is reason, proposition, thought, ground, discourse, argument, and a string of semi- and nonsynonyms. A "technical" point of logic (if, indeed, "logos" understood extensively can be said to be approached "technically") might well bear the weight of a world; Carnap imagined so and Heidegger would make the argument, quite differently, in his essay of 1951 on Heraclitus's Fragment 50, "Logos" (and, with variations of some importance, elsewhere).

Here the matter, for Diano, is this: The Aristotelian syllogism (and this is a broad notion, as it includes Epicurus's poetics and forms of argument as well) is finally ideal, though in a rather special sense. "All men are mortal; Peter is a man; necessarily, Peter will die." The expression remits to concepts (substances with properties, like "man" and "mortality;" the expression "All men are mortal" can be rendered as "All men are in possession of, or participate in, 'mortality'"); it is a formal system of operations upon forms, a syntax operating upon terms remitting to ideas and itself having (at least tendentially) the coherence and longevity of the idea. ("Peter" will necessarily die, but the form of the proposition that expresses this necessity will as certainly not: The form "All x are y; k is [a member of] x; then necessarily, k is y" will not perish. Nor will the operators "is," "is a member of" and "then" or "therefore" or "implies that." Something like a compensatory relation—between the finitude that the content of this most hackneyed of examples of the syllogism expresses, and the unperishing ideality of its form—is on display.) In the Aristotelian syllogism, then, syntax and objects exist in a correspondent and reflexive relation. Tautology is one of the conditions of this syllogism's truth, and a first sort of necessity at work in the syllogism is just such: "'Peter' will necessarily die, because 'Peter' is the sort of thing that necessarily dies."

What happens, though, when the Aristotelian cosmos (of which "Peter," and "life," "death" and "mortality" and the states and events leading from one to the other are different sorts of parts) is taken as the object of the Aristotelian syllogism? That cosmos—that *interpretazione del mondo greco*, that "Greek world"—stands on a chain of causes linked ultimately to an uncaused figure that reflects, paradoxically untouched but touching, on the effects, the motions, of which it is the uncaused, unmoving cause. Offered in *Physics* 8 and in *Metaphysics* 12, the uncaused cause is the eternal signature of the finitude of the causal chain. The figures of the Aristotelian syllogism are of course part of the cosmology that bears that signature—"Peter," and the concepts of truth, life, death, necessity, and so on, as are also the operators "is," "is a member of" and "then" or "therefore" or "implies that": All are effects caused by antecedent causes, and thus signed as finite by the figure of the uncaused cause—but they are also expressions of that cause. They are inhabited by something, a form, other than they. This means, minimally, that every term of the Aristotelian syllogism is both finite and ideal, ideal in its finitude, finite in its ideality. Clearly aware of the seeming paradox that the figure of the uncaused cause entails, Aristotle multiplies arguments both for the necessity of its existence, and for its radical exceptionality—as though by sufficiently isolating the uncaused cause, its disruptive effects on the cosmos, on its ontology, and on its logic, could also be isolated or banished to a separate domain. *Simultaneity, motion, necessity, eternity,* and the signature of *finitude* work hand in hand. Diano gives this interlocking five-fold-form a name. "God," writes Diano,

> is a form, the form par excellence, τὸ τί ἦν εἶναι τὸ πρῶτον [*to ti en einai to proton*]. As form he remains unmovable, outside time, outside space. Moreover, as Plotinus notes, form in Greek, εἶδος [*eidos*], also means "the thing seen." God is, in the full and absolute sense of the word, the "thing" as "the thing seen," in the act in which the very thing itself sees itself understood and understanding [*intelletta e intendente*] as Dante writes.[8] It's a contemplative activity, a νοῦς [*nous*], that takes itself as its object.

Thus Diano on the Aristotelian syllogism, and on the contemplative first form that organizes it. The Stoic syllogism, on the other hand, is not ultimately theoretical: Its necessities are other, and it will not banish the principle of finitude to the numinous region of the contemplating first: of *to ti en einai to proton.* The Stoic syllogism, Diano suggests, falls "back on the 'if' of [. . .] hypothetical necessity that ultimately excludes every necessity and that is established in the pure indeterminacy of the *tyche.*" "Peter will die," yes, but when? The Stoic asks: by what cause? Here a different cosmology, as well as a different sort and series of necessities—distinct from the ultimately theological chain of causes and implications—are entailed. Here, the "pure indeterminacy" of *tyche* might suggest an "interpretation of the Greek world" as a collection or collocation of events arranged, we might say paratactically or anaphorically or rhythmically, around the particle "if"—where the hypothetical syllogism "If Peter is a man, then Peter will die," can be analyzed, for instance, to require a chain of hypotheses that are themselves nondeterminate: "Peter will die, but only if [an unspecified and until the event unknown *m*; for instance, if Peter leaves the house, then he will walk down the street; if he walks down the street, then he will slip and fall; if Peter slips and falls, then he will die]."

Diano is treading on ground turned over, at almost the same time, by the Polish philosopher of logic Jan Łukasiewicz, whose 1951 *Aristotle's Syllogistic from the Standpoint of Modern Formal Logic* (with an important second, enlarged edition finished in 1955 and published in 1957, the year after Łukasiewicz's death) made the distinction between the Aristotelian and the Stoic syllogism in these terms:

The Aristotelian logic is formal without being formalistic, whereas the logic of the Stoics is both formal and formalistic. . . . Formalism requires that the same thought should always be expressed by means of exactly the same series of words ordered in exactly the same manner. When a proof is formed according to this principle, we are able to control its validity on the basis of its external form only, without referring to the meaning of the terms used in the proof. In order to get the conclusion *B* from the premises "If *A*, then *B*" and *A*, we need not know either what *A* or what *B* really means; it suffices to notice that the two *A*'s contained in the premises have the same external form. Aristotle and his followers, the Peripatetics, were not formalists.[9]

For Diano, the Stoic view also excludes the effects of *tyche*; its syllogism, no less grounded in an ultimate cause than the Aristotelian, operates differently: It inscribes this cause within the contingent, hypothetical principles of its effects. The Stoic syllogism, we might say, offers an immanent, rather than a transcendent, limit to the endless en-chaining of causes. The Stoic syllogism is syl-logistic, in the sense that the bringing-together of collocated terms susceptible of our noting that they have "the same external form" regardless of what they "really mean," or whatever procedure is indicated in this case by the prefix syl- (<συλ, with, together), operates on cases; it is radically nominalist;

and it conditions the syllogism's necessity and truth-value to time. Here the conditions of simultaneity, motion, eternity, necessity, and finitude, do not operate in unison, as in the Aristotelian syllogism, but in different registers and to some degree in contradiction. A different account of the figure in which these conditions are joined is entailed. Diano:

> For the Stoics God does not have a form properly his own nor is he separated from things. He is in them as a body is in a body, a fluid body that can be divided infinitely, whose nature is that of fire [*Per gli Stoici invece Iddio non ha forma che gli sia propria, e non è separato dalle cose, è in esse, come corpo in un corpo*]. . . . He does not contemplate but acts. . . . Finding his reason for being in the cyclical, God makes [*realizza*] every moment identical to the being that was. Yet he is also providence, πρόνοια [*pronoia*], and the law, νόμος [*nomos*], that governs him. This is λόγος [*logos*], discourse. Thus, God, who is as the Stoics note all these things, is more than anything else λόγος [*logos*]. Not a νοῦς [*nous*] that sees, but a reason that moves from one term to another. Each of these terms is a verb. An event. (my emphasis)

> Per gli Stoici invece Iddio non ha forma che gli sia propria, e non è separato dalle cose, è in esse, come corpo in un corpo, un corpo fluido, divisibile all'infinito, che ha la natura del fuoco, un "fuoco dotato di arte," e le pervade, e sono esse le sue forme . . . avendo

la sua ragione nel ciclo, realizza ogni istante l'identità dell'essere che era, e però è anche πρόνοια [*pronoia*], provvidenza, e la legge, il νόμος [*nomos*], che lo governa, è λόγος [*logos*], discorso. Per modo che Dio, che è, come essi dicono, tutte queste cose, è innanzi tutto λόγος [*logos*]: non un νοῦς [*nous*] che vede, ma una ragione che si muove e passa da un termine all'altro, e ognuno di questi termini è un verbo: un evento.

Inasmuch as God, as *logos*, discourse, *has* his reason (a word that we can also render, of course, as *logos;* the proposition is then, rather more strikingly, "inasmuch as *logos* 'has' *logos*") in "the cyclical," he makes [*realizza*] every moment "identical to the being that was." Or better: God "in having" [*avendo*] reason, or "*logos*, in having *logos*." . . . We understand: "in having" every moment, identical to the moment-in-the-cycle of which it is a repetition and every being, identical to the being-that-was, before—a being called "Peter," for instance. And above all, God, identical to himself, self-realizing "in having" his *logos* in the cycle. But a nonidentity, or a noncyclical moment of divine not-yet-knowing, not-yet-being-realized, impels this eventual identity of every moment and every being with the moment- and the being-that-was. A resemanticization of the Gospel of John is entailed: The Vulgate's "in principio erat Verbum et Verbum erat apud Deum et Deus erat Verbum" now stresses the modal sense of *verbum* rather than its substantial sense. In the beginning was the verb, not the Word. (And also not the act, the substantivized form of the action or acting: not, as in Goethe's *Faust*, "Am Anfang war die Tat.") Between Stoic syl-logistics on one hand and the cases it brings together on the other, the relation is not one of mutual determination, certainly not the spectral reflection of one in the other or the theoretical contemplation of one by the other. The Stoic relation of the syl-logistic form, or the syl-logistic event, with its eventual "objects" is rather provisional and historical, even a relation of technical accommodation. Each event, the syl-logism and its "object," becomes, syl-logistically, a case of the other. (If the Aristotelian syllogism installs or manifests something like a compensatory relation between the finitude that the content of examples of the syllogism expresses, and the unperishing ideality of its form, in Stoic syl-logistics something like the naming of discreet events instead is at work.)

How then to think the relation between these two syllogisms—and the ontologies each entails? Not to mention the theologies? Two directions for the discipline of philosophy—as contemplative, theoretical, eye-heavy; and as practical, effective, embodied—are outlined. Two for theology as well. (On one hand, a *deus absconditus* indifferent to the world except as the object of his contemplation; something closer to an animistic principle on the other.) Two for the historiography of Western culture—a history animated on one hand by a form subsisting over time, Greek or Hellenistic finally, "Europe" and "culture" drinking over history from Pierian springs; embodied on the other, nominal, case-driven, evental, verbal.

Form and Event: Principles for an Interpretation of the Greek World. We have not thought through with enough care Diano's conjunctions, and the work done by the colon in his title, which masks definitions, arguments and propositions: syllogisms. "There is form" and "There is event," and also: "'Form' and 'Event' are the names of principles for an interpretation of the Greek world." But also: The operator "and" (*e, ed*) is *both* a figure of listing (nominalism is the ostension of cases: this apple, that form, that event, this Peter, that death) and the figure of possible addition ("Form and event are *both* principles for an interpretation; they are two substances of which we can say that, *together*, they are principles for the interpretation of the Greek world"). Diano's argument (here again Heidegger's "Logos" essay will prove a fruitful analog) does not offer—deliberately—a solution to the question how to think the relation between the two syllogisms, or not, at any rate, in the frame of an "interpretation of the Greek world." No third way is on offer where the two paths cross. (The tragic scene is not accidental. Diano elaborates the analysis of *tyche* that we find in *Form and Event* in the years from 1947 to 1952 in relation to Sophocles: his "Edipo figlio della *Tyche*," published in 1952, considers the parricidal installing of *tyche* in the empty place left where the father is doubly absent—unknown, but also killed "accidentally.")

What is on offer in *Form and Event*, however, is a quite radical reinterpretation of what we might call "il mondo europeo," the "European world" of the postwar, by means of the interpretation that Diano offers of the Greek. Consider a phrase that must have been present in Diano's mind as he considered and sought to set aside, or erase, or understand, or interpret, the words that his intellectual father, Giovanni Gentile, "quem magistrum adulescens audivi, colui deinceps ut patrem," had furnished in 1932 to the *Enciclopedia italiana* in the article on "La dottrina del fascismo."

> Like all sound political conceptions, Fascism is action and it is thought; action in which doctrine is immanent, and doctrine arising from a given system of historical forces in which it is inserted, and working on them from within. It has therefore a form correlated to contingencies of time and space; but it has also an ideal content which makes it an expression of truth in the higher region of the history of thought. . . . The Fascist State, as a higher and more powerful expression of personality, is a force, but a spiritual one. It sums up all the manifestations of the moral and intellectual life of man. Its functions cannot therefore be limited to those of enforcing order and keeping the peace, as the liberal doctrine had it. It is

no mere mechanical device for defining the sphere within which the individual may duly exercise his supposed rights. The Fascist State is an inwardly accepted standard and rule of conduct, a discipline of the whole person; it permeates the will no less than the intellect. It stands for a principle which becomes the central motive of man as a member of civilized society, sinking deep down into his personality; it dwells in the heart of the man of action and of the thinker, of the artist and of the man of science: soul of the soul.[10]

Come ogni salda concezione politica, il fascismo è prassi ed è pensiero, azione a cui è immanente una dottrina, e dottrina che, sorgendo da un dato sistema di forze storiche, vi resta inserita e vi opera dal di dentro. Ha quindi una forma correlativa alle contingenze di luogo e di tempo, ma ha insieme un contenuto ideale che la eleva a formula di verità nella storia superiore del pensiero. . . . Lo Stato fascista, forma più alta e potente della personalità, è forza, ma spirituale. La quale riassume tutte le forme della vita morale e intellettuale dell'uomo. Non si può quindi limitare a semplici funzioni di ordine e tutela, come voleva il liberalismo. Non è un semplice meccanismo che limiti la sfera delle presunte libertà individuali. È forma e norma interiore, e disciplina di tutta la persona; penetra la volontà come l'intelligenza. Il suo principio, ispirazione centrale dell'umana personalità vivente nella comunità civile, scende nel profondo e si annida nel cuore dell'uomo d'azione come del pensatore, dell'artista come dello scienziato: anima dell'anima.[11]

Anima dell'anima, soul of the soul. Note the repetition of *forma* in Gentile's prose. This "principle"—singular and indivisible, leading to a singular "formula di verità"—is the form that the State takes when all the forms of man's moral and intellectual life are gathered and summarized (*riassume*) in a form that is not correlative to contingencies of time and space. The internal form and norm of the State-as-gathering-of-forms is the "ideal content" of the superior—that is, noncontingent, history of thought. Gentile's engagement with Hegelian historiography is on display here, though the expression "anima dell'anima" has (in the Christian tradition alone) a rather overdetermined history, Patristic and mystical as well as distinctly secular. A *novena* attributed to Luisa Piccarretta runs "O Spirito Santo, anima dell'anima mia, io Ti adoro: illuminami, guidami, fortificami, consolami, insegnami ciò che devo fare, dammi i tuoi ordini." Analogues in Augustine and in Tertullian exist, but also, extraordinarily, in Bruno (describing a pagan "god of gods" who is the "nature of Nature and … the soul of the Soul of the world") and in Lucretius, throughout Book 3 of *De rerum natura,* but especially 3:276–81, regarding the mysterious "fourth element":

This fourth element is deeply buried and deep-hidden; indeed, there is nothing in our body more impalpable: it is the very soul of the whole soul [*anima est animae proporro totius ipsa*]. Just as the force of the mind and the power of the spirit, owing to the smallness and fewness of their constituent particles, imperceptibly interpenetrate our limbs and every part of our body, so this nameless force, by reason of the minuteness of its component atoms, lies hidden; it is, one mighty say, the very soul of the whole soul, and it is the supreme ruler of the whole body [*sic tibi nominis haec expers vis, facta minutis corporibus, latet atque animae quasi totius ipsa proporrost anima et dominatur corpore toto*].[12]

Lucretius surely lies behind Bruno's scandalous materialization and syncretization of *anima dell'anima*, and both, with many more eventual and evental sources crowding into the scene, lie behind the critique of formality (if we accept Łukasiewicz's contemporaneous way of construing the difference between the Aristotelian and the Stoic syllogism), and of formalism, that Diano mounts in *Form and Event*. Diano writes, as we saw: "For the Stoics God does not have a form properly his own nor is he separated from things. He is in them as a body is in a body, a fluid body that can be divided infinitely, whose nature is that of fire." [*Per gli Stoici invece Iddio non ha forma che gli sia propria, e non è separato dalle cose, è in esse, come corpo in un corpo, un corpo fluido, divisibile all'infinito, che ha la natura del fuoco, un "fuoco dotato di arte," e le pervade, e sono esse le sue forme.*] The Epicurean cosmos flickers up and is apparently set aside (*atoms* are precisely not infinitely divisible). Diano retains but modifies the form of the proposition: *anima dell'anima, come corpo in un corpo*, as a body is in a body. But just *how* is a body *in* a body? How, for instance, is a "fluid" or even an igneous body *in* a body? At least, a body's *form* (its idea, its repeatability, its cyclicity) will be minimally altered; a body with another, formless or not-possessed-of-proper-form body *in* it is something other than it was. A body "possessed" is otherwise determined, and cannot be held to the same end, the same entelechy, as a single body, or indeed to a single end.

And in this way, the fantasy of a determining, self-intending, self-regarding and self-theorizing cultural *form* can no longer be held to animate and organize events across history, or to provide principles for the interpretation of other cultures—Greek or European. Diano's remarkable loosening of the concepts and functions of necessity and singularity shakes not just "the Greek world" and contemporary interpretations of that world, but the West's world today too. Minimally, we will note that the technical, logical point on which we opened, and from which *Forma ed evento* takes its occasion, concerns an interpretation, not only of the "Greek world," but also and profoundly of a postwar European world still lit by Fascism's fires. And still and especially pertinent to the current moment—when alternatives to the hegemony of the market of markets, to the logic and syllogistics of extractive and financial capital, and to the hegemony of the cultural fantasies on which they stand, seem lacking. Diano's extraordinary essay builds principles for a counter-interpretation of the principle that European culture carries, like the soul of its soul, a Greek "principle," Aristotelian or Stoic. These counter-principles work to *un*gather all the forms of man's moral and intellectual life that the State, and the fantastic image of Hellenic cultural hegemony, catastrophically gathered and summarized (*riassumere, riassunto*) in the first half of the twentieth century, and threaten to gather together again today.

FORM AND EVENT

CARLO DIANO

The primary and in large part provisional results of my research summarized here arose almost by accident. It had to do with a technical problem in the history of Greek philosophy—namely, the role the syllogism plays for the Stoics in relation to how Aristotle understands the term. How I take the two terms of form and event (and within what limits) will, I hope, become clear in the exposition that follows. The order in which problems came up is respected and begins at the end only to return to the beginning. If, as Aristotle thought, it is the case that every investigation advances along a path that begins with what is closer to us (and, alas, also with what we already know), the path I found myself following—without knowing in any way where it was leading and guided initially only by chance—might have some value as a method.

When asking what a syllogism is, we immediately think of Aristotle. The well-worn example is Peter, but if you prefer a Greek name, there is Coriscus. Coriscus is a man and, because he is a man, someday he is going to die. Where does such a necessity come from? From the essence in which Coriscus has his form. This is a form that contains opposites, and, as is the case for every form in our sublunary world, the form is not real except as the succession of individuals who over time have taken it on. Individuals come and go just as the leaves of similitude in Homer do.

But when Coriscus dies, how does he die? Aristotle does not know and cannot say because Aristotle is a man and not a god: not even a god knows. In Aristotle's universe no one knows for a very simple reason: the time and manner of Coriscus's death is an individual event and individual events are based in matter, and thus occur because of efficient causes. They avoid the necessity that properly belongs to form, which is the only necessity that holds true absolutely and that allows for prognosis and syllogism. Individual events allow for only one necessity, that of the fact, once an event has taken place and this because *factum infectum fieri nequit* [a thing done cannot be undone]. Not even the gods, as Agathon says, can "make undone things that have once been done."[1] Yet even before the events occur, this necessity is ἐξ ὑποθέσεως [*ex hypotheseos*] and is expressed by "if." Translating from *Metaphysics*: "This man, then, will die by violence, if he goes out; and he will do this if he gets thirsty; and he will get thirsty if something else happens; and thus we shall come to that which is now present, or to some past event."[2] This does not get us very far. At a certain point, the series stops: We arrive at an "if" that "no longer depends on another if," and of the two possibilities that comprise the alternative, ὁποτέρ' ἔτυχεν [hopoter' etychen], will be the one that comes to be. And so? That possibility will be the one that occurs. If you prefer to substitute a name for the verb and to speak figuratively, you might say that the possibility that occurs is the one that chance or τύχη [tyche] wants to have happen.

The Stoics fall back on the "if" of this hypothetical necessity that ultimately excludes every necessity and that is established in the pure indeterminacy of the *tyche*. Yet the Stoics deny that there is *tyche*. They pay no attention to the syllogism that derives its necessity from form. Their syllogism consists rather in two main figures, the first hypothetical, the second disjunctive. An important fact often overlooked: Terms enunciate events and not concepts. Concepts have no reality. The Stoics are pure nominalists: Only bodies have reality—that is, are real—but not bodies as such, which would mean reverting back to form and so re-availing themselves of concept, which is exactly the case for Epicurus. As the Stoics note, bodies are rather a historical reality to the degree in which they are grasped by sense as events, τὰ τυγχάνοντα [ta tynchanonta] as they say.

Thus we have the doctrine that states that only the present is real and that the predicate is always a verb in every judging, even when the predicate arrives in the form of a name. To say that Socrates is virtuous is the same as saying that Socrates practices his virtue. This is how the Stoics will argue that virtue is a body. Where else would we hope to find virtue if not in this Socrates here with us drinking his hemlock? At this point the Stoics' most famous and widely misunderstood categories appear on the scene. First, the subject. The pure and simple "this," which is pointed at, as the Stoics say—with a finger—means nothing other than that of being *hic et nunc*. Next comes the quality that holds sway over the place of the form, though for the Stoics it is always as a historical quality. The example they give is "Socrates!" The third is πῶς ἔχειν [*pos echein*]—that is, finding oneself in this or that particular condition, which encompasses everything that for Aristotle and Epicurus is within the sphere of the accidental. The fourth and final category contains all the others. It is only within this category that the other categories become real: the relation, or the category of reality in action, in which the here coincides with everything and the present with forever (what Chrysippus will compare to the moment in which something occurs).[3] Thus, this Socrates here and now, who is conversing with Callias: that is an event! And also reality.

Therefore, we have the following: If this happens, then this other thing happens . . . or as the Stoics say, substituting numbers for the letters that Aristotle used: If this happens first, then the second happens, because the event exists in time and time is expressed by a number. If this happens . . . As was also the case for Aristotle, this "if" opens a series that at a certain point becomes lost in nothing [*nulla*]. The same is true for Epicurus in his dodgy doctrine of the atom. We recall how for him the atom, while falling in a straight line, unexpectedly strays off course and breaks the inevitable series of causes. Epicurus is not doing anything but using the Aristotelian theory of the accidental. Both of them will argue that if it were otherwise, everything would have to happen out of necessity. The Stoics at this point rebel. A causal series that gets lost in nothing? And why cannot everything happen because of necessity? What happens to the unity of the world (and with it God and virtue) if events do not take place because they have to? And lastly: Every judgment is either true or false. From out of these opposite and contrary judgments, the Stoics conclude that if one is true, then the other is false. Here we find the disjunctive syllogism at work. Tomorrow Dione will either die or not. One of the two propositions has to be true. At all times everywhere. If this were not the case, then neither true nor false would exist, since truth is nothing other than fact.

For the Stoics everything occurs because it has to. The *tyche* is nothing but a name the Stoics allow themselves to use but only in the context of the isolated event, when they do not know its cause. Yet a cause can always be found. And where does the series of causes end? In God. And what is God? God is the first of the efficient causes of action. The same is true for Aristotle, but God moves and is not moved[4] and is completely separated from things, whose existence he ignores. This is because God is a form, the quintessential form, τὸ τί ἦν εἶναι τὸ πρῶτον [to ti en einai to proton]. As form he remains unmovable, outside time, outside space. Moreover, as Plotinius notes, form in Greek, εἶδος [eidos], also means "the thing seen." God is, in the full and absolute sense of the word, the "thing" as "the thing seen," in the act in which the very thing itself sees itself "understood and understanding," as Dante writes.[5] It is a contemplative activity, a νοῦς [nous], that takes itself as its object.

For the Stoics God does not have a form properly his own nor is he separated from things. He is in them as a body is in a body, a fluid body that can be divided infinitely, whose nature is that of fire. It is "fire gifted with art" and it pervades things and things are God's forms. He does not contemplate but acts. He is preeminently "the one who does," τὸ ποιοῦν [to poioun], and if as body God occupies space, his actions take place in time, while his being coincides with acting: Space and time are thus one because reality is event and therefore history—that is, the history of God's epiphanies. Before it is only him and then gradually, "walking on his path" as Zeno puts it, he makes himself cosmos. Afterwards he reabsorbs it in himself and sets fire to it. The final conflagration.[6] God returns periodically to do that which he has done, and the series of events returns, always the same. The eternal return. Because necessity means identity, and identity in movement cannot be given except in a circle, which both moves and does not, one and continuous, in which every point, as Heraclitus said, is beginning and end.

This God is the principle of a reality consisting of events. He himself is event, the linking of events, εἱρμός [*heirmos*], and inasmuch as he is [*heirmos*] (as the Stoics were wont to say by employing a false etymology, εἱμαρμένη [*heimarmene*—"the spun thread of destiny"[7]], he is fate). Yet this is no blind fate. Finding his reason for being in the cyclical, God makes every moment identical to the being that was. Yet he is also providence, πρόνοια [*pronoia*], and the law, νόμος [*nomos*], that governs him. This is λόγος [*logos*], discourse. Thus, God, who is as the Stoics note all these things, is more than anything else λόγος [*logos*]. Not a νοῦς [*nous*] that sees, but a reason that moves from one term to another. Each of these terms is a verb. An event.

With this in mind we can now understand Aratus's still-to-be-explicated proem to *Phaenomena*. "From Zeus let us begin; him do we mortals never leave unnamed; full of Zeus are all the streets and all the market-places of men; full is the sea and the havens thereof; always we all have need of Zeus."[8] The streets, the squares, the sea, the ports, but not earth and water and the air we breathe, nor fire, the four elements, and the forms to which the four elements provide matter, but rather the places where people move and where they meet each other, where they arrive and depart, where they find themselves face to face with the event—the places where reality is revealed as event. Just as every proposition exists thanks to the verb and the verb is defined by the event, Zeus, as the beginning of all events, is also the subject of all of our discourses. Every verb that comes out of a mouth implies him. He, precisely, is the one who, without revealing his name, we cannot leave unnamed.

Form and the contemplation of form the God of Aristotle, and θεωρία [*theoria*], contemplation of forms, science. Event and the cyclical, the providential joining up of events—this is the Stoic God and reason or discourse of events [is] science, λόγος [*logos*]. On one hand, we have the categorical syllogism of the form that ignores events. On the other, we have the hypothetical syllogism of the event that ignores forms. And thus, what Aristotle did not know and so could not say to Coriscus, can the Stoics say it to him? They will not say it as philosophers, but rather as fortune-tellers and astrologists because divination—which had no place in Aristotle (and still less in Epicurus) who thought it useless and even harmful, regardless of whether it was true or false—plays a central role for Zeno as well as for Chrysippus.

Here I think we can make out something no one else has—namely, the historical background informing the attitude of these two philosophers. In *On Fate*, Cicero, while responding to Chrysippus, will write: "Well then, here is a specimen of the observations of the astrologers: 'If (for instance) a man was born at the rising of the dogstar, he will not die at sea.'"[9] "If" . . . In Assyrian-Babylonian works of divination, omens are always introduced by the conjunction *shumma*, which means "if." Does the Stoic syllogism originate here? Zeno was Phoenician. Timon called him "a greedy old Phoenician fisherwoman."[10] Chrysippus was born in Soli in Cilicia, and his father was from Tarsus. They had read these books and they certainly had seen how fortune-telling could be employed syllogistically. Cicero's later testimony was no mere coincidence.

Yet this is not really the point. Even if it were just a coincidence, the psychological (and thus historical) principle that explains it is actually the same for both: understanding reality as event. Stoicism descends from it and forms of Semitic religiosity largely lead back to it. Only in reality-as-event can divination be explained and nowhere more than in Mesopotamia does it take on such monumental importance.

To finish up with ontology, which was revealed by logic, here is another fact even more important than the first. In the Babylonian conception of destiny one finds not only events but forms as well. It is a god who establishes the nature of the thing together with the name. And it is a god who can always change it, because destiny is a decree that always updates itself. This form-destiny is called *nam*. "The Babylonian *nam*," Giuseppe

Furlani writes, "is a preliminary sketch of φύσις [*physis*] and of the Aristotelian εἶδος [*eidos*]."[11] No, we are light years away from Aristotle: The Babylonian *nam* is the first hint of the Stoic φύσις [*physis*] in which the εἶδος [*eidos*] is quality and not substance, and is rooted in time, and is identified with the event. It is only that their god, unlike the god of the Babylonians, does not hear prayers and cannot be swayed by offerings. Having been translated through the Greek categories of being, this god has hardened into a will that cannot be altered throughout eternity.

In his great work on the stoa, Max Pohlenz reexamined the problem that Edwyn Bevan had posed earlier[12]—namely, the features in Zeno's and Chrysippus's works that allow us to recognize the original mentality of their race. Pohlenz will lay out a number features. Our response has already been given: What the two philosophers contributed as the decisive characteristic of the ethnic and cultural sphere to which Zeno and Chrysippus belong was their understanding of reality as event.

They contributed their insight at a specific moment when the event had begun to dominate Greece. It was not a simple case of Greece actually ignoring that reality is an event. That idea is a part of shared human experience, part of its Mediterranean origins. Greece had faced that insight about the notion of reality as event and won it for the first time during the Homeric epoch when Greece had barricaded the insight away in the fortresses of its aristocratic warriors. For a time, Greece managed to contain it in the sixth century B.C., bending it to the law of the cities Apollo and Athena had protected, when, as it dramatically reappeared again, much like the giant Antaeus, born of the earth at the moment, the understanding of reality as event threatened to overwhelm Greece. Then Greece drove it back beyond the sea along with Xerxes's hordes in the fifth century B.C. The Greeks celebrated the victory of the Olympian gods together with their own.

At this point the forces that had allowed the Greeks to resist were largely spent and outside circumstances had weakened their defenses: the Macedonian hegemony; the pressure exerted on the periphery by the various great states of the time, which were emerging from the dismemberment of Alexander's empire; the instability in which Greece's continual wars weighed down the future of public and private life; the slow but noticeable penetration by ethnic groups from the East (which was due to how much of the political and cultural boundaries of the Greek world had been extended, thus opening the way to them while also providing them with weapons). The great age of Hellas had come to an end and the age of Hellenism had begun.

All of the facts historians enumerate to describe the new era stem from the category of the event: there is individualism in which formal difference gives way to existential and numeric difference; a generic and simply quantitative universalism that is its necessary correlate; the use and abuse of the title "Savior," given to the gods just as it is given to men; the making divine of all those who were seen as messengers of the event—the quintessential examples were to be found in princes; the vogue surrounding the cult of Asclepius, the new god of miracles; the abandoning of more Hellenic divinities for the more esoteric and soteriological ones of the East; the gradual decline of the anthropomorphic conception of the divine and its substitution of the concept of force with that of substance; syncretism, of which such a concept forms its rationale and origins; the belief in demons; the return to vulgar forms of superstition and the spread of magic; and lastly divination, which was of course based on the occult, magic, and astrology. The single most important cause, however, that is able to define this changed vision of the world, is the hypostatization of the event as such—that is, as *tyche*.

Let's take a closer look at *tyche*. *Tyche* is the point where various conceptions of life encounter each other and then radiate outward. The word is aoristic—that is, names the fact in the moment of its occurrence. Thus the verb that corresponds to it is always in the aorist tense. This distinguishes it from μοῖρα [*moira*], which has its verb in the perfect tense εἵμαρται [*heimartai*], and which, in its less rigorous form, is normally found (though not always) in the *Iliad*. There *tyche* presupposes, unthinkingly perhaps, the idea of a necessity decided upon beforehand. When this necessity is rationalized in the concept of a preconstituted order, to ἀνάγκη [*ananke*] (which Homer was already aware of), the perfect participle is added, εἱμαρμένη [*heimarmene*], which, understood to be a technical term, later drops the noun (*ananke*). At this point it takes on of course the value of a name.

Tyche as such does not appear in Homer's poems. It does appear for the first time in Hesiod as a personification, one of many, in which forms are distinguished through which the workings of the divine are made clear. From Hesiod up to the fifth century, wherever *tyche* appears as a subject, it always refers to divine action (what will be the term's very own presupposition). Once it has been made explicit as an idea, *tyche* appears in those expressions in which the gods, or better the god, "Zeus," and then very frequently, δαίμων [*daimon*], with which it is usually identified, are combined with the name under the form of an authorial genitive.

Toward the middle of the fifth century in Athens, *tyche*, thanks to Anaxagoras, is separated from the gods and then begins to negate them. For Euripides the dilemma is whether something occurs on account of *tyche* or the gods: "If there is *tyche*, we do not need the gods, but if the gods have power, *tyche* is nothing."[13] For the first time in the history of Western thought, man has to face the concept of chance. It is a concept that, as a remainder of a negation, is rendered as tautology: To say that an event, which is to say a *tyche*, had as its cause not the *tyche* that Zeus or the other gods possessed, but now on account of the *tyche* alone, is the same as saying that the event happened because it happened and thus did not have any other cause except itself. Such a perspective was not lost on the Greeks, which found its expression in a new term, the αὐτόματον [*automaton*]—that is, "that which from itself" [*il da sé*]. In the *Physics*, Aristotle, taking into account how the term was being used, will say that the *automaton* belongs to the chance events that take place in nature and the animal world. The *tyche* for its part belongs to the world of man.[14] Yet, given that there are events that do not occur with a view to their own end (and thus forego the necessity of having a form), such events have as their ultimate principle nothingness and so produce themselves from themselves. Thus the two terms are brought together in one definition in which the *automaton* is genus and *tyche* the species.

In the fifth century, *tyche*-chance is the word the Greeks will adopt though its use is limited to educated men. People know nothing of it, the proof of which is found in comedy, where there are no examples. In the fourth century, *tyche*-chance descends among the crowd, but the crowd transforms it and makes a god out of it, Fortune. In reality the concept of chance, of the event that has no cause, or better, of a cause that operates without any view to its own end, can be held on account of reason: Emotion [*sentimento*] rejects it and with it popular mentality. For emotion, the event is always cloaked in mystery, referring to a power that transcends it: the *tyche*-goddess! Philosophers and poets of the new comedy, based as it was on the ideas of philosophers, object. "In Tyche we have no deity, no, no!," Philemon of Syracuse will have one of the characters say.[15] "But what happens of itself (*to automaton*) to each of us, that we call Tyche." But this is how Aristotle defined it! So be it. In any case, next to the statue of the *Tyche* rise up those of *Automatia*, of the "From Itself!" The *tyche*-goddess preserves the illogical, momentary nature of *tyche*-chance, but is seen as more a cause of good than evil. Often this is expressed, with apotropaic intention, by the adjective ἀγαθή [*agathe*]: This was the only reason that *tyche* was made a god. The "Good *Tyche*" is substituted (but not without a change in tone) with "The Good *Dèmone*." And just as there is a personal *dèmone*, so too is there a personal *tyche*. It has its official form in the *tyche* of kings and cities.

After *tyche*-chance and *tyche*-goddess we have *tyche*-destiny, which closes the cycle of forms that clothe the event. In *tyche*-destiny any hint of indetermination is gone. There is no difference between *tyche* and *heimarmene* ("the spun thread of destiny"), except the one that the subjective character and the particular nature of the event have with regard to the law that accounts for it and that manifests the universal and objective order out of it. *Tyche* returns then to its original meaning, when as τύχη θεῶν [*tyche theon*], it names the momentary quality of necessity personified in the *Moira* (the Greek goddesses of destiny and fate), a necessity that the gods made sure came to pass. Thus *tyche* came to be identified with the will of the gods themselves. "*Tyche* and *Moira* give everything to man," Archilochus sings.[16] And later Sophocles will write: "*Tyche* does not intervene before *Moira*." The problem is that in the perspectives of these two poets, the gods were still referred to as persons and not as the iron-clad chain of causes that the Stoics had reduced them to (with the Stoics the *tyche* came to be thought together with *heimarmene*). *Tyche* only became a part of a shared idea later, but, as one might expect, when it did, it lost much of its rigor as a concept. We have an important example in Horatio's odes to Fortune, where *tyche*, although lining up with the notion of *serva Necessitas*, always remains a god, and as such, is the object of the poet's prayers.[17]

Chance as *tyche*, goddess as *tyche*, destiny as *tyche*. Three interpretations of the event, three attitudes, three visions of life. Let's begin with *tyche* hypostatized as Fortune and made a god. *Tyche* is the event as momentary and contingent fact. Who or what is the god exactly? We already raised the question when we were discussing the logic of emotion and describing the process through which *tyche* is born. It is a power [*potenza*]. After the discovery of Melanesians' *mana* (and what was found to be similar in other primitive religions), the concept of power became the center of modern inquiry. One tried to put it in relation—as their principle motor—to the various forms through which religious experience is represented. If we ask where the representation of power originates, one answer might be in the "distress" experienced when faced with anything that "takes you by surprise" and that we experience "as essentially other." Obviously, if the more or less established and conscious representation of power is effectively the response to the question that is contained implicitly in "distress," and if the "taking by surprise" and sense of "otherness" are nothing but elements of the "distress"—then the process is missing its founding principle. It follows that if the concept of power is therefore empty, every deduction that begins here—and therefore every "because"—is impossible or arbitrary. Every deduction has to depend on other categories, which, so as not to be deduced from the phenomenon [of power] itself, are hypothetical and in fact beside the point. This is exactly what happens.

Let me make a banal argument. For what or who is power a thing? Because it is effective, no? "A thing is *mana*," explains a Hocart island villager (I am citing Gerard van der Leeuw's book *Religion in Essence and Manifestation*), "when it is strikingly effective; it is not *mana* unless it is so."[18] Alright then, what power operates, what is it? What is it for me, not what is it in and of itself? How and where does it operate in the course of my life, as it marks out, even slightly, an interruption or break? Choose any name you want. I am going to adopt the name the Greeks employed and say: *tyche*, an event. It is the thing as event that takes us by surprise, that appears to be different, that makes us see an action of a power dimly and that also underlines that a god is at work. All of us have had and continue to have this experience. To linger a bit longer with the Greeks, the examples one could cite are in the hundreds. Why bother though? None of them have the weight of the one given us by the *tyche*-god, and this because *tyche* here is the bare event [*nudo evento*]. It is what thinking, freed from the gods, had pushed from the universal into the realm of the singular and contingent of the factual. And a female god was made from this *tyche*.

The event is contingent and singular; contingent and singular is the representation of power too, which is precisely how *mana* is represented. Therefore, we need to begin with event, which as a concept is just as empty as that of power, and which, as a matter of fact, is always related to someone and as such is always distinct. It is determined by the subject and not by an unknowable object. It is determined in the forms of lived experience conferred on each, depending on one's attitude and the historical conditions within which one's existence takes place. This fact, while it allows for deduction, makes event an entirely phenomenological category, where power is already understood to be an ontological concept, and, separated from the principle that determines it, is empty and remains empty.

It has been said that the Hellenistic Age was one of conflict. The most important one was undoubtedly between the world of culture and religion. Yet these worlds, each taken on its own, continually open to contradiction, which then reveals even more conflict. Historians speak of involution and try to find the causes in external circumstances, more often than not throwing up their hands and giving up the search for a single cause. Yet that cause exists and it can be found in the constitutive principle of the event, against which form has already faded. In the solitude of Chaeronea, completely dominated by the power of the event, Plutarch will be the last to contemplate form; after him there is not anything but event. The new era had already begun—our era and it started with an event: the child-god, out of whom the Mediterranean had created a fable even before he was born. The son of a mother, a mother of flesh and blood. He too was made of flesh and lived and then died among men too. Later he rose and then lived among them again.

We could express the difference between the world of culture and religion badly by using the terms reason and belief. If for reason one understands the discursive faculty, in no area more than in that of belief does it celebrate its greatest orgies. Generally, reason is not what holds the world together, the world we think is real, and what preserves the shape of things. Culture, for its part, when it challenges religion, has to depend less on the system of syllogisms and more on insight. Without getting off track by introducing a topic that could take us far afield (and that is not useful given the small number of facts we have to go on), we can see how each world, that of culture and of religion, reciprocally mark the limits of the other, despite their different nature.

In the world of religion, if one abstracts from cults and symbols that the force of tradition preserves, to a certain extent, unchanged, there are two extremes. On one side we have the conception of the divine that we find in the singular and contingent forms of primitive mentality. On the other, we have the speculative and dogmatic systematic character of the Mysteries more generally. In one of them is the individual isolated in the chaotic sphere of multiple powers; in the other, the individual as member of a society of initiates who identify and recognize themselves in the cult of one power. On one side, the dark woods [*selva*]; on the other, the church. Their respective principles are the same: event and power. They each have the same goal: salvation. Yet the principles and the event of the first are singular and limited to the moment, whereas those of the second are universal and take eternity as their setting.

Dark woods [*selva*]. At the center lies Fortune, without form or figure, even if sculptors have made statues of it. Around it we find a jumble of demons and anonymous "forces" in persons and things. Mankind does not have anything but a weapon, and that is magic. The Church: In the temple, professional priests are subjected to only one rule: You must attend to the divinity. The divinity has form, yet it is a symbolic form in which are joined the two supreme events of the world and mankind: birth and death. Generally speaking, the divinity is a goddess, a mother, whose son or lover dies and is then reborn. Salvation arrives in the consecration of man to the god [*nume*] through a ritual in which he dies and is reborn. He dies to the tumultuous and murky world of events and power and is reborn in the luminous and peaceful world of a life in which the precarious nature of forms and the instability of the event are annulled in the mystical identity of the principle governing both.

Moving from one extreme to the other, however, the separation between dark woods and church is not so clear-cut. There are a series of degrees through which the various forms of religious experience, the more they lose contingency, the more they acquire the characteristics of universality and unity. At the center, much like a summit, where the first pole converges and where the other gives way, lies the terror of a fate written in the planets and stars whose science goes by the name of astrology. All of these various degrees of separation can be found in the same person just as they can be found in the religiosity of every age.

If you want a more complete picture, reread Apuleius's *The Golden Ass.* Here is the story of a man who leaves the dark woods for the church, who, beginning his life as a donkey—that is as a mere servant of Fortune—penetrates into the changeable world of the event through magic thanks to his "fatal curiosity"; into the freedom of rebirth in the mystical death in the Mysteries of Isis. Psyche too suffers from just such a "fatal curiosity."[19] The fable's meaning transcends the laws of genre with which it is presented. This is a curiosity that, despite having the same logic, is precisely the opposite of what we find in Lucius. Lucius loses his form because he had wanted to act during the night of the event. Psyche loses the event because she, during the night in which she alone was given as the bride of Eros, contemplates his form with the light of a lamp. The principal cause of her misfortune is to have been the bearer herself of form: her beauty. Furthermore, with regard to form, the cause will be found in her curiosity, in wanting to see beauty enclosed in the box (*pyxis*) that she carries up from the subterranean Proserpina to Celestial Venus. In this final task she surrenders to death. Yet in death, she makes out two lives separated by the Mysteries. She again finds Eros, in the inexpressible sphere in which power resides; a power that is the principle underlying both forms and events.

The divinities of the Mysteries almost all originate in the East, but what about the Hellenic? What about the gods of Pindar, of Homer? These are gradually transformed into powers and fused with the new divinities of the event. Those whose mythic forms are not transformed (even if they maintain their cults and festivals) live on only in poetry and art. The most important divinity of this impulse toward revolution or, if you prefer, of this dynamistic involution that tends toward unity, is a new divinity born under Ptolemy I Soter, at the expert hands of Eumolpidae in Athens: Serapis who combines in his person Zeus, Dionysus, Osiris, and Apis.

Culturally speaking, if we consider this in the mirror provided by philosophy, we can make out three groups. On one side are the Aristotelians, the Epicureans, and the Cyrenaics. On the other, the Cynics and the Stoics. Between the two groups are the Academicians and the Skeptics. Letters and the arts as well as class customs that carry on the more explicitly Hellenic traditions will generally be found with Aristotle and Epicurus.

The Cynics and Stoics reproduce the previous two perspectives we located as the opposite poles of religion and they do so in reason. As was the case of man in those religious Mysteries, here too we also find the man of the dark woods. In the same way, we find a Cynic lurking in the Stoic. As Aristotle teaches, the opposite term will always be found within the same genre. Both the Cynics and the Stoics ignore forms and take their cue from the event. Yet for the Cynic the event is separate and emptied in the immediacy of the fact. For the Stoic the event is the moment of a cyclical process. A verb in divine discourse.

The event in the immediacy of the fact. The Cynics do not believe any power lords over us. They pay no attention to God but not so that they can reason about it. It does not matter if Fortune or God actually exist. Reality will always be this and only this: a fact. They only believe in one power and that is I. An I without a face, empty, just as the event that calls the I forth is empty and reveals it: a will laid bare, in the same way that the event is pure necessity—that is, the suddenly felt necessity of the fact. It is the I that the event reveals because I is the event itself that does so. The event individualizes, which explains why the Hellenistic Age is precisely the age of individualism.

Yet individuation is different across periods. It depends on whether the event is a fact or Fortune, or God. Alexander and Diogenes; two individuals. According to many, it is the difference between the elect and the marginal. In Alexander, the son of Zeus, the new Heracles. In Diogenes, the son of the bare fact. Diogenes is also Heracles but he revels in the name of dog. The one and the other are two invincible wills. But Diogenes's will is stronger because it negates. The Cynic's life is absolute negation. That is its virtue. It is a negation that links man to the dark woods and then within that clears a space for his freedom.

The freedom of the Cynic is as empty as his virtue. For its part the Stoic's freedom still means something. Events do not happen randomly but rather add up to a totality: They take shape with an end in mind. Necessity is not found in the fact but rather in providence and reason. Freedom will be found in identifying oneself with this reason. Listen to Cleanthes:

> Lead me on, O Zeus, and thou Destiny,
> To that goal long ago to me assigned.
> I'll follow readily but if my will prove weak;
> Wretched as I am, I must follow still.
> Fate guides the willing, but drags the unwilling.[20]

Virtue. Events do not happen randomly but every event can be found here, right now. God is in every event, just as the circle is found in each of its points and in each point the circle both moves and is at rest. God is always here, now, for someone, for me. Action cannot be put off. Each of us has his or her own virtue. No one can take another's place, and that is true whether it be king and servant or friend and friend. Besides, the virtue of one is the equal of the virtue of the other, but that is also true for who is at fault. Degrees of who is at fault are all equal because all events necessarily must be so. Duties too.

Events are necessary and necessity is providence. Is every event therefore necessarily good? Not in and of itself but in the connection the event has with other events. Neither good nor bad, the event is fact. Good and bad reside in judging and in the action produced by that judgment. The Stoic, like the Cynic (though for different reasons) is indifferent to the event. The Stoic, without pleasure or pain, desire or fear, does what reason tells him to do: *si fractus illabatur orbis impavidum feri-ent ruinae* [Should the round world break and fall about him, its ruins will strike him unafraid]. If he is unable to act, and if his death can serve as an example to others, he will take his life by his own hand. He too is invincible.

What does reason tell the Stoic? Simply that man establish in himself and in his life with others the unity that is proper to it—that is, the solidarity that resides in the cosmos, which the point shares with the sphere. Where the Cynic is anarchic, the Stoic is a citizen of a city whose walls encompass a world that is both Greek and Barbarian. The cosmopolis. Where forms are pared down to the event, no distinction between races or nations will be found. The event that individuates, universalizes. Where this universality is empty, there you will find the dark woods. Where universality has content, there is the cosmopolis. The city of the Stoics is universal in the same way that the church of the Mysteries is universal.

When Stoicism came to Rome, it made sense of the city's history and created a content for its empire. The poem of Rome is the *Aeneid* and its hero is a hero of the event. Still, enmeshed as he was in Alexandrine poetics, Virgil found a place for the Homeric gods there, which explains the poem's disharmony, from which Virgil is unable to rise above. Lucan attempted to write a poem capable of completely following the poetics of the event, but he was no Virgil. If you want to find the

Stoic "here, now," one both singular and total, punctuated and continuous, look for the vaults and arches where unity is mediated in relationship and where space moves with time. A cyclical time that encompasses and encloses the world: Roman architecture.

The world of religion is the world of "trepidation" and "dread." The world of Cynic and Stoic philosophy is the world of the will sealed up in negation or of a will made tense by effort; a world without smiles and without rest; a world that pays no attention to the Graces and the Muses. The Graces and the Muses, smile and rest, are to be found in the world of happenstance. Aristippus, Epicurus, and Aristotle inhabit this world. Given that it is the world of happenstance, it is also the world of forms. Weak and shadowy forms like the event from which they distinguished, but forms nonetheless.

From Aristippus to Epicurus to Aristotle; from the smallest to the largest. For Aristippus forms exist—and here note that Aristippus does not live except through forms. Forms are the luminous foam of the instant, the illustrious and risky game a poet plays. His quickness is the equal of the sheer giddiness of his inspiration, which he invokes and which he then scatters into nothing. This poet is chance. It is a capricious and ironic poet who plays and is generous but only with those who play. Life is nothing other than a game, played in scenes in which the stage and masks are constantly changing. Aristippus accepts each and every mask and is able to be himself gracefully behind each; a man who lives by art and in art, *non inconcinnus* [in no inelegant fashion] as Horace writes.[21] A Cynic once reprimanded him for having made philosophy a comedy. "Yes" was his response, "but I act for me and not for others." For comedy and the game, but especially for pleasure; a pleasure that Aristippus is able to regulate accordingly, because he is the one who seeks pleasure. If you tell him that the scene in which he is playing is made of wood and canvas masks, he will tell you that the forms constructed out of them do not actually consist of wood or canvas. If there is nothing behind them, nonetheless they are forms. They actually exist.

Yet every game is risky. Aristippus for his part is not afraid. He knows it is the price one has to pay to play. If he thinks about death, he hopes for the kind of death Socrates had, but not because it was Socrates who died, but because Socrates knew how to make his death beautiful. If you want an inverted example of Socrates, take a look four centuries later at how Petronius died. Aristippus did not have many disciples and so his influence ended quickly. Not everyone has the capacity to live as if the forms that reason sees as unreal are actually real and so the event reverts back once again to the brute necessity of the fact. One of the last of Aristippus's disciples, Hegesias of Magnesia, was in fact a propagandist for suicide.

In one of his letters, Epicurus writes: "It's absurd to run towards death because you are tired of life, when it is your manner of life that has made you run towards death."²² Epicurus does not want to play. If the game has risks, then he will not play. Moreover, he does not concede that forms might be the appearance of an instance, which is to say that something has to be there that is at rest. Not everything can happen by chance: There has to be necessity too and somewhere in between a place for freedom as well. Chance gives us the possibility of moving where and how we want. Necessity insures that the earth does not give way beneath our feet; it allows us to walk in any direction. Thus, Epicurus amends Democritus and adopts Aristotle's theory of substance. He founds the stability of species on *aeterna foedera naturai* [the eternal covenant of nature] and declares that forms are eternal. Forms are eternal not only in the same way that species are, but also in the way that individuals are—in gods who exist between one world and the next and so avoid falling prey to disaster: all equal, all beautiful, all blessed. In what does their beatitude consist? Only this: that they do nothing and fear nothing. To do, which is born out of desire, and to dread, happen only when the event is sovereign. Also, in *intermundia*, no events exist. Lucretius avails himself of Homeric images and words. Remember that Epicurus's gods are the same as Homer's, having been transformed into one single form and made wise.

Mankind can make such a condition possible and live a mortal life among immortal goods, while staying within the limits of the necessities that bare existence requires and drastically curtailing the space in which the event occurs. Said differently: If pain is knocking at flesh's door, man can withdraw to the fortress of the soul as his final refuge. Here are preserved in memory the images of the first good things he experienced. In defense of daily life and protected against the surprises chance holds in store for him, he will take his inter-mundial seat in a garden outside the walls of the city, far away from the crowd and their commotion. Here he will meet his few friends and they will share opinions and ideas—good or bad, noble or plebeian, it does not matter. What does matter is that the opinions and ideas are Greek, because only the Greeks are capable of wis-dom. Few in number, they agree to form a pact. As is true for every human society, friendship originates in a pact founded on what is useful. Yet it moves well beyond any pact because friendship is beautiful in and of itself and because pleasure loves company. Eyes reflect in other eyes; hands hold other hands. "You're here too! And you too! And grace flowers, χάρις [charis]. What about death? When it comes, it comes, but right now, there's no death. There's just me and as long I'm here, I'm going to enjoy today. Seize the day!—*Carpe diem*. Today is gone, maybe death will be here and maybe you won't. Today ends, but a day is truly a life. A day, an instant, an eternity. They are all the same."—In the realm of form, oh Epicurus! Exactly. Of form, because form is the ground from which he looks out while he laughs at the sea of the event: form, only form resides outside of time.

For Epicurus form is a means. To find a form that is an end in itself, we need to turn to Aristotle and before him to Plato. Plato separates form from earth and because he does not know whether to remove any sort of meaning from event or not, he opts to neutralize it in the number and theology of the Mysteries. And Aristotle? What is form for him? We already saw it when speaking of the unmoved mover. It is "the thing seen." Knowing [*conoscere*] is seeing in the fact. On the lowest rung this is represented by the senses, and the preeminent sense is sight. Its culmination is intellect. The intellect, *nous,* is an eye, the eye of the soul, as Plato calls it.[23] The eye sees the universal, whereas the body's eyes can only see the particular. Just as the eyes of the body require light, so too the intellect. Another intellect within intellect illuminates it in the same way as the sun.

The eyes see bodies. They see them as figures and they transmit their image to the imagination, a faculty that lies between sense and intellect. The intellect finds the universal in this image. What was a figure for the eyes becomes form, εἶδος [*eidos*], in the full sense of the word. This is the key point. What is the difference between figure and form? It is the difference between the particular and the universal says Aristotle.[24] What does universal mean when the form is as visible as the figure? The risk is that one may slip into abstraction and take form as species. It is a risk that Aristotle does not shy away from although his actual experience of the question will not be found here. Aristotle was educated in the Platonic school, and like Plato was Greek, and thus distinguished precisely in the following: the sense of reality as form, an enormous eye that opens onto the world and that forever projects images of it.

The figure and the form. Let me begin by telling you that form for Plato is ineffable and as such cannot be taught. One sees or one does not. Countless people live and die without having seen it; philosophers are no different. The simplest among us can see it given that the clearer it is, the greater the level of simplicity required to see it. Whoever does see it, sees it suddenly, as an act of grace, ἐξαίφνης [*exaiphnes*], as Plato says. He or she sees it in the figure, the same figure that, at a moment's notice, appears to be separated from the subject that it had marked before precisely as subject. Form appears to reabsorb space within it and to be outside time. Artists are the ones who see it the most. Indeed, they are artists inasmuch as they see it. Afterwards they carry it over from the living subject who up to that point had made an event of it, into an inert subject, using any kind of material, be it marble, bronze, or canvas, in order that we see only it. Plato does not know how to understand it except as separate; he sees it outside the world, outside the heavens, in another heaven where no storms and no events light up the sky. We really must not separate out form, however, because once we do, either figure returns (which in turn demands another form), or if it does not, then what you have is not actually figure or form. I can say this somewhat differently. A Greek statue from the end of the sixth century or from the first half of the fifth century—the Attic *kouros* of Munich, for example, or the statue of Apollo of Olympus—has a halo draped around it, much like a luminous nimbus, which creates tension around the limit while at the same time encloses it and makes an absolute thing of figure, the αἴγλη [*aigle*]. Homer and Pindar will see the gods circumfused by it. This absolute thing is form, but it is not eternal. Rather it comes from within, from the center, and then returns there.

Aristotle can see this nimbus but winds up separating it from the subject just as Plato did. He constructs a separate subject out of it without figure while for the subject that enjoys a figure, he leaves the species in place of form: "And when we have the whole, such and such a form in this flesh and in these bones, this is Callias or Socrates; and they are different in virtue of their matter (for that is different), but the same in form; for their form is indivisible."[25] Aristotle cannot see that both Socrates and Callias might be a form (and not matter plus species). The individual remains therefore contingent and, similarly to Oedipus, the son of *tyche*. Just as individuals are history, history is the reign of *tyche*. Where there is no *tyche*, there is no history. In the heavens there is none because motion has the immobility of the identical there. Beyond the heavens, there is none because form is pure activity, the bare and abstract intellect of the unmoved mover. In man's intellect there is none, despite the fact that paradoxically it is more resolute than the divine (because in addition to seeing itself, it sees forms and reflects the world), but does not have (though in actuality it does) another difference that does not consist of number. And it is the contemplative leisure of such an intellect, removed from the upheavals of history and the effort of acting, that Aristotle, in a conclusion he shares with Epicurus, will invite man to withdraw into himself. The intellect is the final Mount Olympus of forms, luminous yes, but also lifeless because these forms are separated from bodies and thus are no longer substances as Plato had once viewed them. These forms do not set Eros in motion and thus do not draw on life. When Aristotle was accused of impiety, he fled the trial for Chalcis. He said that he did so as not to give the Athenians any opportunity to sin against philosophy a second time.

Outside of the intellect in the world of bodies, form is species: a degraded and generic form, on whose empty foundation chance has traced the marks of the individual, the event against which man from the moment of his birth struggles and in whose sphere life unfolds. There is no need for intellect here. Aristotle has to employ the word φρόνησις [phronesis], which is to say practical wisdom, something that lies between wisdom and cleverness. The slave knows how to use it better than the king; so too the practical man more than the philosopher. Having to choose between knowledge and practical wisdom, Aristotle will write in his *Ethics*—thus preparing the way for Epicurus—that it is better to have less of the former and more of the latter.[26] Thus virtue is a compromise, the median between two extremes. The golden mean is always difficult to measure, given that what is fair for me is not for you. Generic form or species plus chance, and with chance the will that wavers between the Scylla of pleasure and the Charybdis of pain—together they form character, the ἦθος [*ethos*], that is the ensemble of habits with which a species descends to the species below, the multicolored and changeable outward appearance that is draped over the nude *tyche*.

You can construct for yourselves the poetics that emerges from these elements. Either there is a figure that substitutes the halo of the form with the smoothness and sparkling features of a surface: thus Callimachus's hymns. Or there is a species that wavers between necessity and contingence: This would be the universal constituted by what is possible according to necessity and what is plausible, which is to say a play of characters in a succession of events guided by chance. This is the new comedy we associate with Menander. Why comedy? Because as form degrades to species, the event is emptied of any value in relation to chance, and chance is one of the Muses of the comic. A comedy that, precisely because of this, does not laugh but only smiles because it is a comedy of half forms, just as the event is a half event. If you want the laughter that scorches the heavens and the earth, you need Aristophanes. With him the event is a god; it is Dionysus-Phales, the cosmic god, the god of the victorious life in which the principal actor looks like a hero. There are no gods here and the principal character is Davo, a good-natured servant. Good-natured comedy smiles. Sometimes she cloaks herself in sadness because under all of the half forms there is the I, an I that is the same for everyone—*homo sum!*—just as the event transformed into chance is now the same for everyone. This I is the child of nothing, similar to the event that lays it bare. The nothing here is death. The smile sharpened by congeniality: *philanthropia*.

To the Alexandrians, Menander's comedy seemed the mirror of life and it was: a mirror of their life, much like an epigram that highlights the moments in the oval of a cameo. It is similar to Herodas's *Mimes*, and partly to Theocritus's bucolic poetry—only partly because in Theocritus's other poems he had located the ancient soul of the Mediterranean in the Sicilian shepherds. It is what we find so surprising and enchanting in the paintings in Knossos and Hagia Triada. In the midst of the haze and marshes of the Mincio, Virgil captures the music yes, but the colors, no.

The form not separated from its subject. The Homeric gods and heroes, of the *Iliad*'s Homer. Pindar's gods and heroes. Phidias's gods and men:

race of men, one race of gods; both have breath
of life from a single mother. But sundered power
holds us divided, so that the one is nothing, while
    for the
other the brazen sky is established
their sure citadel forever.[27]

Over and over it has been said how these gods are eternal forms. The ancients said the same thing. Again and
again it has been repeated that man was conceived as an
idea by the same Greeks who also venerated these gods.
Yet the meaning of these forms and the power of this
idea remained only at the level of intuition; it still
remains for us to sketch their logic. What has been done
up to now—and the classic work in this regard is Walter
F. Otto's *The Homeric Gods*—is marred by two defects.[28]
First, Otto forgets that the gods only exist in man's representation of them and that such a representation is
naturally bound to change. It does so not only according to period and subject, but precisely changes in the
very same subject, according to the situation in which
the subject finds himself or herself. Thus, a theology of
individual divine figures is constructed, which the his-
torian will reject and the philosopher will find of little
use. Second, beyond form lies the event. As soon as
form moves, the shadow of event appears and no divinity is entirely a divinity of form, Apollo included (even
if he is the highest expression of form). Why? Because
as god, Apollo bears both death and healing within

him; because as the god of prophecy, Apollo is the god of the event. If there are principles, at least in part, that underpin the logic of form, those for event remain to be elaborated.

Yet—and this is the most important point—form and event need to be thought as pure and simple categories, and as phenomenological and not ontological ones (to do so would mean to do metaphysics in vain). We need to articulate these categories but only on the basis of the phenomenon and thus historically within the sphere of attitudes and situations that are reflected in them. With this in mind, the history of Greek gods coincides and is identified with the history of Greek religiosity, which in turn contains the entire history of the Greek spirit. This centuries-long history needs to be researched and then reconstructed from the works in which that spirit is expressed across different moments. It is only in these works that we can locate again their lived experience in the form that it had in that instant, which is the only meaningful and real form. This will be a history in which philology and literary analysis, research into the political context and the study of monuments, as well as the philosophy and the science of religions will need to work together, meeting up in a process of analysis and synthesis.

The terms of such a discourse do not allow me to discuss even generally how the Greek spirit unfolds from Homer to Socrates in the workings of these two categories. I can, however, sketch some principles, with the warning that the generalizations that I will be using must be understood as limits. So too those principles, which on one hand aim at clarifying a concept, must on the other hand ignore the entire complex of differences within which the historic individual is bound and moves.

Form and multiplicity move together: where there is a form, there is no reason why there cannot be another form even if it is identical. Aristotle gives us the best example. After having demonstrated the oneness of the first mover (using the principle of individuation as the basis that he had located in matter), he multiplied the number of unmovable movers by the number of spheres. He understood that such a demonstration of the oneness of the first unmovable mover would be needed only to the point at which the form was taken to be species and not as substance. The gods of form are many and on the basis of the limit that every form contains, there cannot be but many. To divine unity one ultimately winds up at the logic of the event. The distinct theologies of the Epicureans and the Stoics confirm it. For Epicurus the gods are forms and so are many; indeed, they are infinite, just as worlds are infinite. For the Stoics, who use the category of the event, the world is one and the one is God. The gods, having passed the Aristotelian examination of substance—this is what Cicero said about the Platonic idea—have only one form. The other has a thousand forms, as many forms as there are events that celebrate their epiphany.

The opposition that we find between these two theologies—in the age whose feeling they reflect—lies between a traditional and a new faith. In the altered attitude toward spirits, traditional faith is gradually substituted by the new. Analogously (though in the opposite direction), we find it at the origin that separates the polysymbolism of the Mediterranean religion taken as one and the Olympic pluralism of the Greeks. The logic of the event utterly dominates the former: Forms are multiple, but are understood differently from what their figure represents. In other words, they have only evocative and symbolic functions. At their heart— and this is just as is true for the mystery cults—is a goddess, a mother "of many names," as Aeschylus says about Earth, "and of one essence."[29] She is the goddess of life and death, the lady or mistress [*potnia*] of mountains and water, of animals and plants, both oracle and sorceress, tutor and warrior. She is represented as a human, which is her principal and more significant form, but she is also seen as belonging to the animal, vegetal and inanimate realms. These representations change according to the ideas concealed in her metamorphoses and in her actions.

Next to her though subordinate (which is required given her originary, androgynous character) is the *paredros*, who is also polymorphous, and is symbolized variously as son, brother, or lover, depending on the cycle of birth and death. The mistress brings together within her godhead the principles of permanence and transience in the doubled figure of mother and daughter, a figure kept alive in the historical age is the set of forces that distance themselves from the rhythms of the world over which she reigns.

For the Greeks this fluid and ambiguous world of transposed concepts and symbols divides and then is fixed in the univocal singularity of the figures. Figurative meanings give way, the multiplicity of representations become the multiplicity of substances. For the first time things leave the magical sphere of the event and are elevated by the scattering and instability of accidents to the immobile unity of being, and reduce their whole invisible essence to the visible surface. It is a world of forms that arises and with them for the first time space appears, separated from time, into whose flow the event is now drawn. The result is that existential experience and primitive mentality confuse space with time: space as the limit of the form that it creates, outside of which there is nothing, which we know was true for Greek art. Aristotle will define the space "in which the world" as he says, "is with regard to its parts and not with regard to the whole," whereas for the Stoics, space is external to the world and is defined by the event.[30] Reality is exorcised. The plot of sympathetic relations on which the magical operates is broken; the realms of nature divide; movement and force return within the limits of their own size. Actions no longer occur at a distance nor are there any metamorphoses. Power [*le potenze*] leaves the sphere of visible things, over which man can now dominate. Power descends into the depths of the earth, into the abysses of the sea. The gods of form are separated from the epiphanies of the event.

The gods are now all anthropomorphic but remain immune from old age and death. They are motionless in an age without time: The nimbus that encloses the figure of man is made substance and projected into eternity. In the sphere of the eternal the mountain that had once belonged to Potnia and to her theriomorphic *paredroi* rises up; for the Greeks that had come from Thessaly, that was Olympus;

> With that
> the bright-eyed goddess sped away to Olympus, where,
> they say, the gods' eternal mansion stands unmoved,
> never rocked by galewinds, never drenched by rains,
> nor do the drifting snows assail it, no, the clear air
> stretches away without a cloud, and a great radiance, αἴγλη [*aigle*],
> plays across that world where the blithe gods
> live all their days in bliss.[31]

This is no light of the sun but the light that Plotinus will announce as being inseparable from form. It is visibility that constitutes the essence of form; the light of Greek plasticity that is internal to form. Beyond time, the gods let the event fall outside, so that the event either has only the void, the inverted necessity precisely of the *moira* that is juxtaposed to the gods, or the event is lost in the general and impersonal representation of a daemon without figure. That which is in the logic of the principle to which the gods owe their beginning and all of Aristotle's metaphysics confirms this. If the thing is a "thing seen" which is to say form, the accidental properties of a thing will inevitably fall outside substance, with the result that the event will enjoy only the necessity of the factual. This is expressed in *tyche*. Only now can we see why Aristotle's movers are unmovable and Epicurus's gods inactive. Inactive too are the gods of whom we are speaking. Freed, therefore, from the necessity that is in things, if they act, they do so for pleasure. For the first time man contemplates pure action in the gods, that has the end in itself, that returns to itself and is play; that action that the Greeks revered in their agonistic encounters, and what Aristotle will make the only proper form, as pure *energeia*—the action in which man is free; the only path to science.

Because they are in complete possession of themselves and because they do not suffer from fatigue or need to be healed, the gods "enjoy all of their days," and they belong to "the easy life." They are the quintessential "blessed ones," so too the exemplary "immortal ones," "the celestial ones." Above them Zeus commands, but his rule differs from Potnia's since his is the dominance of a form and not of power. His rule is founded on visible and external force and not on a force that is either internal or invisible. His rule is always pitted against something or someone, and this is almost always nominal, because forms are absolute and exclude control (and control is a remainder of the logic of the event). When forms are completely subordinated to Zeus, there will no longer be forms but events and Zeus will no longer have a figure. Zeus, a god, and not a goddess.

This too is in the logic of the form for the reason that the event does not exist except to the degree that, and in the act in which, it is generated, evokes the idea of the mother and thus belongs to the feminine. The form, however, is the only one that exists and exists for itself. Form is essentially virile. Athena, who is one of Potnia's representations, and to whom tradition awards maternity as well—she was once taken into the sphere of the Olympian gods—becomes the Virgin par excellence and is born from Zeus's head. Dionysus, on the contrary, is the eternal god/son and is continually found among women. He himself is feminine. In all agrarian-based religions (always event-based), the first and oldest figuration of the divinity is feminine. Thus the foundation for all oracles is the Earth and Themis is her daughter. It is the majesty of form that Apollo and Athena defend against the Erinyes, the revengers of maternity and the event in Aeschylus's *Eumenides*. As long as Greek civilization remains faithful to forms, it is virile and glorifies beauty in the figure of man. It will represent what is nude in god and ephebe, reducing to a minimum the sexual markers, while the maiden and the goddess it veils. Only the Hellenistic Age will revert to the nude goddess of the Neolithic and more advanced Paleolithic Ages and in both life and art the feminine will dominate the Hellenistic Age—the age of the event.

If the opposition between a unitary world of the event and the pluralistic world of form resides in the analogy of its terms with a change in direction—the same opposition between event and form that runs from the beginnings of Greek civilization to the final Greek age—then the process of unification, brought on by just such a process, will dovetail with the religious revolution of the sixth century B.C. As was the case with the Hellenistic Age, it will coincide with political revolution. In both periods philosophical speculation competes with plebeian superstition. And as is the case in the latter period, the overarching direction is represented by the event in the forms of *tyche*, the *heimarmene*, and the mystery cults, much as it did in the prior period. There the goddess-*tyche* corresponds to the *tyche* of the gods; to the *heimarmene*—who is both reason and law—corresponds *moira* [Fate], both providence and justice; and to the mother gods corresponds Demeter; to the god who is born and who dies corresponds Dionysus. It is Dionysus who erupts into the world of forms and upsets them—a god whose symbol is a hollow mask, the empty and fragile form that the event takes on across its changeable features.

Direct from the countryside where the lords had exiled him, Dionysus brazenly enters the city and takes up residence there, dragging onto the stage, in front of the orchestra and his dancing goats, the Homeric heroes. He strips them of their regal cloaks, tears off their faces, and makes masks of them. Under that mask he shows man made bare. Dionysus teaches that the man that is in all, is nothing. Tragedy: the revolution of the age of tyrants. And the very same Dionysus, in the figure of Phales, takes the man of the countryside [*gleba*], pulls him drunk onto the court of his ithyphallic followers, and there frees him in the ecstatic joy of the Komos [a ritualistic drunken procession performed by revelers in ancient Greece and typical of Dionysian rituals]; from the animal to the human, Dionysus teaches man all of the forms through which the event magnifies the force of life in the world. Dionysus makes man the absolute victor; man, who represents this very same force in its most original and lowest expression—in the bowels and genitals—is raised to a victorious symbol of life. Dionysus provides him with it in the lewd maxim, in the shameless invective, a weapon that frees him. Dionysus has man touch the adjacent heights of what he had made man feel in the hero's tears. Comedy: the revolution of the age of the people.

Within the terms given and the changing yet converging limits of inspiration under which Homer wrote, the *Iliad* and *Odyssey* are distinguished by the Hellenic divinities of form and the pre-Hellenic divinities of the event. In both, the supreme divinity is of course the same—Zeus. These are the poems of the Achaean nobility. But in the *Iliad* Zeus is subject to the empire of form and for the most part is kept at arm's length from the event. In the *Odyssey* he truly is the divinity of the event and we only see bits and pieces of his form. Similarly, the *moira* in the *Odyssey* is always the *moira* of the gods, whereas in the *Iliad* (except Canto 24, which marks the passage from the world of the one to that of the other poem), *moira* is outside their purview or is juxtaposed to them. And while in the *Iliad* the dominant divinities are male, in the *Odyssey* they are female: one goddess alone, Athena, watches over the action. She is the ancient goddess of the palace, tutor to the king; the goddess who in the historical age will mentor the city. Her final transformation, in the Hellenistic Age, will be into "the *tyche* of the king"; in the city itself that bears her name, the "Good *Tyche*." During the period of Lycurgus of Athens, the "Good *Tyche*" received a part of the offerings, where before it was Athena alone who had received them.

The hero of the *Iliad* is a hero of form and thus of force; there can be no other relation between form and form except through force. The form is absolute and excludes mediation. Relations of force yes, but this is not a brute force whose beginning and end reside outside itself, which is true for all the forces of nature (and thus concern event). It is the force of action whose end is in itself, the force that is proper to form. In its effects it is as much a material force as the other. It is βία [*bia*], given its principle cause. It is also Κράτος [*Kratos*], and it is *maiestas*. In Hesiod *Kratos* and *Bia* are *paredroi* to Zeus. In Aeschylus's *Prometheus* they are his ministers.

As the expression of individual superiority (thanks to the dignity that form confers on it), this force is ἀρετή [*arete*]—that is, excellence or virtue. Its companion is glory, κλέος [*kleos*], in which this force is reflected and continues over time (even if in its struggle with event it will give way). The reason is that form is absolute and indifferent to event. This explains why Pindar wanted form to be honored in one's adversary and why Homer honored form in the defeated (and thus the agonistic characteristics of archaic wars and the importance that the Greeks gave the games). Celebrating the Funeral Games in Honor of Patroclus after Hector's death, Homer revealed the essence of that war in the games as the Achaeans understood it and so gave us one of the keys for reading the poem. And if the Redemption[32] provides some catharsis in the logic of the event, the Funeral Games provide it in the logic of the form. Catharsis is double. The first is Dionysian and thus reveals the foolishness of forms to man and that the event cannot be undone. Man in turn is steered away from the contradictions and limitations of the multiple to the calm, undifferentiated and infinite of the one.

The second is Apollonian. By elevating forms to the punctuality of the eternal, Apollonian catharsis separates form from time while proclaiming the event null. The first is tragic, the second epic. Euripides will contrast the forms of catharsis one to another in the *Bacchae* and in *Iphigenia at Aulis.* In his history Thucydides will end the "high tragedy" of the Athenian empire in epic.

If the hero of the *Iliad* is one of form but also force, then the hero of the *Odyssey* is a hero of the event and as such is a hero of intelligence. The reason is that form is without mediation but the event is completely caught up in mediation. And here too we need to distinguish between the two because just as the force of form will be found in its cause, *kratos*, and not *bia*, so too this intelligence is μῆτις [*metis*] and not νόος [*noos*]. It is an intelligence that calculates but does not contemplate, that does not stand still but moves, that has no other object except the doing. It is the intelligence that later will be called σοφία [*sophia*] and φρόνησις [*phronesis*], ξύνεσις [*xynesis*] and γνώμη [*gnome*]. Aristotle will define it, in contrast to intellect and science, as the faculty of calculation and reasoning. He will name it τὸ λογιστικόν [*to logistikon*], using, without realizing it, the idea found in the name to which the etymology of *metis* refers—namely, measure. Moreover, as reasoning—that principle common to both practical and poetic activities—is made specific in prudence or φρόνησις [*phronesis*] and in "art" or τέχνη [*techne*]. This is not art as we understand it, what the Greeks called music (and which has to do with form), but rather technique [*tecnica*]. Similarly, prudence falls under the same genre of πανουργία [*panourgia*], or being clever, and so belongs to *metis*. Its hero is Odysseus because he is both prudent and clever, and because he is the creator of things [*artefice*].

When it comes to prudence, Odysseus is above all Διì μῆτιν ἀτάλαντος [*Dii metin atalantos*]—that is, "equal to Zeus in *metis*," but chiefly he is what Zeus, as we shall see, never is: πολύμητις [*polymetis*]—that is, of the multiple *metis*, a "mastermind."[33] As such, at least in part, Odysseus is ποικιλομήτης [*poikilometes*], "of a *metis* that always changes colors," while in other respects, he is πολυμήχανος [*polymechanos*] "rich in expedients"— that is, of τέχνη [*techne*]. When Odysseus meets Alcinous, the first thing he does is mention his clever tactics [*inganni*]. Thanks to one of these (and not his excellence [*arete*]), he is πτολίπορθος [*ptoliporthos*], the subverter of the city. As for the arts, there is no weapon or contraption that he cannot handle. He can do everything, from constructing a raft, which he uses to leave Calypso, to building his own bed.

There is one thing he does not know how to do, though, and that is play the κλέα ἀνδρῶν [*klea andron*], the songs of heroes on the cithara, but not because he somehow lacks *metis*. Rather, *metis*, the fertile inventor of "arts," is infertile when it comes to art. Among all of the epithets of the Muses, you will not find one that reminds you of Odysseus. The Muses want a contemplative mind, not a calculating one. Hermes invented the lyre but it is Apollo who plays it. Odysseus does not contemplate. In order not to fall victim to the "spells" of the Sirens, who also sing of nothing else but the exploits of heroes, Odysseus will tie himself to the ship's mast. And if he does not plug his ears with wax, it is out of *philomathia,* which is proper to *metis* and not out of any love for contemplation [*theoria*]. Not a part of who he is, the song cannot not have any effect on him except as an outside force of demonic powers. Moreover, when he hears them sing of his exploits, his κλέος [*kleos*], he weeps.

Weeps, because in his world form is nothing other than an element of the event. Glory is an illusion. The only reality is "sorrow": Odysseus is precisely the one who "suffers many sorrows."[34] He narrates them yes but does not sing about them. He narrates them, one after another in chronological order. "What shall I tell you first? What shall come last?"[35] Events belong to time and connect to each other, forming a chain. Only forms exist in isolation and are outside of time, thus the story-like and boundless style of Oriental and later Roman art, as well as the contemplative and delicate style of Greek art. The very same Homer has both: the staccato style of the *Iliad* and the legato style of the *Odyssey.*

The intelligence-*metis* of the event. You can see it in the gods. They hold it as what is properly their own:

Cronus, Prometheus, Hephaestus, Athena, Hermes. All gods who, either because of their origin or function belong to the sphere of the event. In Cronus, ἀγκυλομή-της [ankylometes], metis is cunning. In Hephaestus, both crippled and ambidextrous (πολύμητις [polymetis] and κλυτοτέχνης [klytotechnes]), who does things with two hands that the hundred-handed Hecatonchires cannot, and yet is deformed so that he "catches the swift Ares too late," metis is technique. Metis combines both technique and prudence in the πολύμητις [polymetis] Athena, Metis's direct daughter through Zeus, whose polymetia, as a poet from the fifth century B.C. will note, would amount to nothing if not for her hands. Quintessentially cunning and occasionally practical is metis in Hermes, who like Odysseus is πολύτροπος [polytropos] and δολομήτης [dolometes]. He is the god of all roads and all unforeseen events, trickster and thief. Yet in Prometheus metis is prudent, cunning, and practical. Continuing we note that just as the kratos of the form is to the bia of the event, and the noos to the metis, so too does one find metis associated with the bia in the Cyclopes, who combine vigor and violence with the μηχανή [mechane] of work. One of the Cyclopes, Brontes, is married before Zeus to the goddess who bears the name Metis. The Cyclopes are the direct prog-eny of Uranus and Gaia. It was the latter who first devised a "fraudulent art" against the "violence" of her husband. The Cyclopes have as their close relatives the

Hecatonchires, who, with their hundred hands and fifty heads, are nothing but pure and dense *bia*.

It is just this dense *bia* of the Hecatonchires that Zeus must use in order to defeat the Titans, but he does not do it on his own nor on his own initiative. Rather he does so on the "advice" of Gaia. Not having been born with *metis*, he adds it later, when, now king, he marries and swallows Metis, the daughter of Oceanus. Here as before names speak. This *Metis* has close sisters, *Eurynome* and *Telesto*, which is the same as saying *Imperium* and *Auctoritas*. These features (along with *Consilium*) belong to what is royal and so come to define regality. Yet Zeus, if he is preeminently μητίετα [*metieta*], is only so with regard to *consilium*—that is, βουλή [*boule*], and therefore inasmuch as he is king and thus to the degree that as the supreme divinity, he is god of the event. But he is never πολύμητις [*polymetis*] and even less ἀγκυλομήτης [*ankylometes*], as are Cronus and Prometheus. And if Prometheus, with his *arete*, can do anything, πάντων πέρι μήδεα εἰδώς [*panton peri medea eidos*], Zeus only knows about the things that are proper to immortality, ἄφθιτα μήδεα εἰδώς [*aphthita medea eidos*]; things outside of time and that, removed from the event, are unchangeable and belong to what is of one. This is the knowledge of form, the only knowledge that Aristotle will give to his static Intellect. This is a knowledge that is purely theoretical, whereas for the Stoics the *logos* is both practical and technical.

Do you want to see this Zeus of the form in all his majesty? Look at him when he stands on the summit of Mount Ida and contemplates, never moving a finger:

> And all were blaming Zeus with his storming
>   dark clouds
> Because the Father decreed to hand the Trojans
>   glory.
> But the Father paid no heed to them. Retiring
> peaks apart from the other gods, he sat aloof,
> glorifying in his power, gazing out over
> the city walls of Troy and the warships of
>   Achaeans,
> the flash of bronze, fighters killing, fighters
>   killed, κύδει γαίων [*kydei gaion*] . . .³⁶

This explains why Zeus—who is invincible and who possesses both *bia* and *kratos* in their doubled nature (his scepter and his lightning bolt), on which he founds his reign—is so prone to falling into clever traps and why he is so easily seduced and tricked, all of which he obviously hates. He loathes the arts too, because they change the form of things, and, his "advice" notwithstanding, this is why he is set off so often in the *Iliad* from *moira*, against which he is helpless.

The genius of Aeschylus observes this Zeus in *Prometheus* and, as we have noted, unties the knot. On one hand, there is force in all its majesty, conferred on it by form; on the other, intelligence in all of its variety and multiplicity, which belongs to the event. It is the intelligence that Aeschylus had heard Anaxagoras, researcher of meteorites, of λαμπάδες πεδάοροι [*lampades pedaoroi*] glorify, as he reminds us in a passage from the *Choephori* still to be fully understood. Aeschylus takes from Anaxagoras, who had pointed out that the three key elements of mankind's progress were to be found in an intelligence (perfected by hands), in time, and in the event reduced to the bareness of *tyche*. Man, not progress, is the most terrible of all the things on the earth and sea and in between.[37] But as Zeus's power is mindless and has to submit to the event, so too is Prometheus's intelligence weak: He has to submit to Zeus's power (Prometheus is the son of Gaia-Themis, the keeper of all events). Ultimately, they will be reconciled, but Zeus remains superior to Prometheus, who in his ring and the willow wreath carries the marks of his ancient punishment. The reason lies with Aeschylus who is a Marathonomachos and, like Achilles, has a lion's heart and Achilles's eyes. He believes, beyond any thought of the justice of the event, in the justice of form, just as Pericles did and as Thucydides will later.

As much as Odysseus needs *metis*, Achilles has no use for it. He never acts with the event in mind and the action borne in him does not arise from any prior deliberation, but rather out of passion: from rage, the only passion that properly belongs to form; the rage that Aristotle defends and that the Stoics struggle against. If the action of the form is forceful, its guiding principle cannot be anything other than force. As this force does not have the wild, potent quality of the event, but rather the force of the form conscious of its power and able to bring together that force within, so too does this force belong to the rage that generates it. Thus form judges according to its own standards. When Achilles is about to draw his sword against Agamemnon, he stops himself. The poet then has Athena intervene, but Athena is not anything but the *arete* of Achilles now made goddess. Only once does Achilles's anger get the better of him and it happens when he faces Hector. But he is wounded in love and love is one of the cosmogonic forces of the event. It is here that the *Iliad* crosses over from epic to tragedy.

Achilles's rage finds its reply in Odysseus's patience, πολύτλας [*polytlas*], just as he is also πολύμητις [*polymetis*]. Never does Odysseus become angry though this does not mean he says no to vengeance. In fact, only Odysseus's vengeance is truly authentic, τίσις [*tisis*], in the Mediterranean sense of the word, which is to say premeditated, cold, ruthless. Instead Achilles acts recklessly and in the heat of passion and then ultimately lets himself go and weeps with Priam about the nothingness that is man. Furthermore, while Achilles's vengeance is subjected to the laws of form, and is a duel, a contest [*agone*], with equal force of arms on both sides (which he faces knowing that, whether he wins or loses, he is risking his life), Odysseus's vengeance is orchestrated through trickery, a deceit that the contest provides. Moreover, it is not a duel but rather a massacre that he sets in motion, but only after he has arranged everything and is certain, with Athena's help, that he will survive. Another fact is also decisive: Achilles fights using "a lance and sword," the weapons of *arete*. Odysseus for his part kills Penelope's suitors with a bow, an insidious and dubious weapon that does not require any *arete*. It is a weapon that strikes quickly and invisibly just as the event does. It is the weapon that the Greeks gave to their Asiatic Apollo and his sister Artemis because they were "the carriers of death," but that the Greeks always believed to be contemptible and considered barbarous. Troy is captured through deceit and by the bow because the *moira* had desired its destruction and had nothing to do with the work of *arete*. Furthermore, the bow also belongs to Heracles, who, like Odysseus, is pre-Hellenic and a hero of the event. Yet he is a hero of *bia* and not *metis*. Therefore, even before drawing the bow, Heracles uses the club; his bare hands are "lethal," which is the case for all of the children of Gaia. Separated from the *kratos* and without the support of the *metis*, this *bia* cannot be anything but lowly and blind. Moreover, Heracles is condemned to servitude for the remainder of his life. When he is not carrying out his labors, he goes mad: He is both patient and crazed, just as Odysseus is patient and wise. The Cynics and the Stoics make out of him a hero of duty but the hero of Aristotle, the Greek, is Achilles.

The hero of the *metis*, Odysseus is also quintessentially eloquent. It is not the eloquence of Nestor, singer of "glories" who, lost in memories of times past, exhorts his listeners with examples and sings (λιγύς [*ligis*], *canoro*, a technical term) as the Muses, the daughters of Memory, sing, and whose words, like those of the Muses, are "sweet" with a true sweetness in no way mixed with "honey." Instead, Odysseus's eloquence is completely directed at the present and aims at only one thing, the event. Like the event it is also ambiguous and changes color, enveloping and soft like snow: μειλιχίη [*meilichie*] and κερδαλέη [*kerdalee*]—that is, "benevolent-looking and slyly intent on gaining its advantage." This eloquence is the counterfeit of the Muses' song, which is why it was banned from their chorus. Such eloquence makes colors fade from the Muses' singing, just as the false makes truth fade. The patron of eloquence is Hermes and like Hermes, it charms and captures souls. It is what Achilles hates most:

> I hate that man like the very Gates of Death who
>> says one thing but hides another in his heart.
> I will say it outright. That seems best to me.[38]

He does not do this out of any ethical consideration but because he follows the law of his own nature. If the event is always different from what it appears to be, the form, in which being and being seen coincide, is all surface, on one plane: that which appears frontally and is the "only seen thing" of archaic and classical sculpture.

You always see Achilles from the front, "square-shaped," much like in the statues of Polykleitos's *Canon*. Odysseus, however, is always slanted, πολύπλοκος [*polyplokos*], "all perspective and spiral-like," similar to the octopus depicted on the Minoan jug from Gurnia and in the simile by Theognis of Megara: πολύπλοκος [*polyplokos*] and πολύτροπος [*polytropos*], which is visible across all 360 degrees, in four dimensions. The same will reappear with Lysippos during the Hellenistic Age, when form gives way to the event, and space, once again outside, will be joined to time, when space will light with shadow.

Yet, while the Hellenic Achilles is essentially sculptural and names Ephebian statues that will keep alive his image across the ages, the Mediterranean Odysseus is most certainly pictorial. We ought to look for him more in *The Odyssey Frieze* of the Esquiline Hill and less in the rotating *Ulysses Grimani* housed in the National Archaeological Museum in Venice, which is one of the rare statues we have of him. These paintings, Roman and no longer Greek, are illusionistic, where the forms lose their substance in the contingency of space; an open space that gives every point the instant's capacity to come apart from one moment to the next.

Space and time, light and shadow, in the dialectical unity of what is continuous. Color, the illusionary visibility of what is continuous, in the fluid and frightening liquid that wraps round the event and in which every apparition is possible and every miracle real: metamorphosis and magic. This is the environment in which Odysseus moves, in which the monsters whom he fights against live; in which he defends himself against the magical seductions of the goddesses, of Phaeacian ferrymen carrying, you do not know, men or souls; and finally the atmosphere Odysseus creates when he returns to his island and around his profaned house. On one hand, he can assume any form, like the Proteus of his sea, to whom has been revealed the secret of every event. Like Athena who guides him, he is always disguised and bears up under the laughter and the beatings of Penelope's suitors while in the guise of a beggar. On the other hand, there is Achilles for whom any sort of transformation is impossible because the space that he carries inside is static and outside of time. The light his figure gives off is indivisible. Therefore, he has but one form, like his gods, and never, even when facing death, does he agree to outfit himself in Thersites's rags. Yet Achilles dies young because the form, in the impact with the event, breaks because it cannot change or be made pliable. Odysseus, changeable and flexible, follows the event here and there and dies an old man. And their two deaths are antithetical, just as their two lives are. Each conforms to the logic of the principles they obey: Achilles encounters death with open eyes and chooses it freely, while Ulysses is killed by his son,

Telegonus, by mistake, the one "born in a distant land," whom Ulysses had never met.

Achilles and Odysseus are the two souls of Greece and the history of the Greeks is their history. Both merge and are sublimated in Socrates. Socrates has Odysseus's intelligence and Achilles's strength, but he dies like Achilles, consciously accepting death, looking it in the face, so as not to lose form; he thinks of Achilles when facing the judges who will condemn him. For Achilles form is his mortal figure made eternal by fame and glory, which he contemplated on the cithara when he sang of the exploits of heroes. For Socrates form is law, the laws, νόμοι [*nomoi*], of his homeland. He sees them enter his narrow prison cell, at the solemn moment of the test; he sees them though not as images of concepts spun out by reason, but as real essences, flesh and blood creatures, and with a flesh transubstantiated by light, in the αἴγλη [*aigle*] that covers forms; in the same way that Achilles had seen his gods, with the same eyes, beyond description; eyes that only Plato will have among Socrates's disciples.

Before Socrates, Euripides's heroines had died on stage for form, just as Achilles had. Euripides, the poet under whose gaze *moira* will empty out in *tyche*; Euripides who had seen the gods of form disappear into the ether. But form was in his heart, form that had no other substance save that of his poetry, an appearance, a trace.

For this appearance Iphigenia dies, the young Iphigenia, in the era in which one still believes in appearances. The aging poet had dedicated his most beautiful poem to youth, to her and to the Graces, bound everlastingly to the Muses, the same Muses who keep watch over the sepulchers. They immortalize in song the glory of the form, in the night of death, in the luminous glow of form, in a place beyond the rocky sea of events.

The night of death is also the night in which life is generated. Hesiod makes her—that is night-Nyx, together with her brother Erebus—the daughter of Chaos, from whose union Aether and Hemera are born. Plotinus will put One out of which the Intellect originates in the place of Chaos, the luminous and transparent world of forms, and three times removed, the Soul, the dark and ambiguous world of events. The One, what is beyond form and event, ineffable without figure, where one can say only that it is motionless and without thought—Being coinciding with Nothingness.

for Pietro de Francisci

You write:

> In religion there is a point where the two moments
> join, what is called ritual inasmuch as it is the form
> for staving off or for causing events. The same is
> found in law. Should we emphasize events more than
> forms or are forms more important? Furthermore,
> are not forms thought as being essential, especially
> in earlier, primitive periods, precisely in those peri-
> ods in which humanity shakes when it encounters
> contemporary power?[39]

Here is the crux of the problem and everything depends
on how we define the two categories of event and form.
I will say that, based on my current research and on the
basis of the results that I arrived at in terms of event, I
can offer some thoughts. I did want to repeat again here
what I lay out in my essay—namely, that I award a
purely phenomenological value to these two categories.
We make history and not metaphysics. What one can
deduce for metaphysics from my reading is another
matter, but that has no place here.

Let's start with event. Event originates in the Latin
and translates, as is often the case with Latin, the
Greek word *tyche*. Event therefore is not *quicquid*

èvenit [whatever happens] but rather *id quod cuique èvenit* [that which happens to each one]: ὅ τι γίγνεται ἑκάστῳ [*ho ti gignetai hekasto*] as Philemon writes, recalling Aristotle.[40] The difference is crucial. If it were to rain, it is something that occurs, but that in and of itself does not make it an event. To be an event, I have to feel that such a taking place involves me. And yet, if this event appears to consciousness as an occurrence, then we know that not every occurrence is an event. Commentators have always misunderstood this distinction, found in Aristotle too, when examining *tyche*. Aristotle limits events only to the human sphere. He also declares that not all occurrences that exclude necessity, which is proper to nature and art, are ἀπὸ τύχης [*apo tyches*] but only those that man presumes need to have an end in sight, which is to say, that take place for him. Remove the interpretation of the universe that belongs to Aristotle and you have *tyche* in all the depth of meaning it has in Greek language and experience. In these it will appear sometimes as chance, other times as goddess, still other times as destiny, and in the era farthest removed from us, as the unerring manifestation of the divine, the τύχη θεῶν [*tyche theon*] or ἐκ τοῦ θείου [*ek tou theiou*].

Thus one cannot speak about event without considering its relation to a given subject, and to the domain of this subject. Moreover, seeing how it is within this relation and out of such a domain that the occurrence—

about to be constituted in event—is revealed to consciousness as a true and proper occurrence, not only can occurrences be experienced as events, but so too can those we refer to as "things." These are the forms that man has directly in front of him, in the act in which he or she perceives the event's existence as something that may be for him or her and not for the form itself. This explains the indistinction between name and verb that, according to glottology, appears in oldest periods of language and that we find in many primitive languages (though not only). The ancient Stoic teaching that sets forth the essence of the proposition in the verb and believes the name to be a secondary thing—whereas for Aristotle ἄνθρωπος βαδίζει [*anthropos badizei*] is the same as ἄνθρωπός ἐστι βαδίζων [*anthropos esti badizon*]—finds its primary justification in the linguistic perspective of Zeno and Chrysippus, both of whom were Semites.

Inasmuch as it is *id quod cuique èvenit*, the event always takes place in the *hic et nunc*. There is no event if not in this very place where I am and in the instant in which I perceive it [as taking place]. Let's say lightning strikes a tree during the night. I see the tree in the morning. This fact, if it is to be an event for me, is not an event inasmuch as the *evènit* is actualized in an *èvenit*, and the tree is not simply one among many points in space. Rather it is actualized in the *hic* in which I find myself. We know that one of the means through which primitive people seek to ward off the event is by willfully ignoring and consciously not seeing the place or the thing (where what constitutes an event for them occurred). The same thing happens to us albeit in muted form.

From the preceding it is clear that *hic et nunc* does not localize or define the time relations of the event, but rather that the event defines the *nunc* in time and localizes the *hic*. Furthermore, the *hic* occurs as a consequence of the *nunc* because the former functions as an interruption of an undifferentiated line unperceived in its duration, which is to say is experienced as a duration within existence as something lived. The event emerges here and imposes itself. It is on account of this interruption that the *hic* is felt and then revealed. The distinction that scholars of primitive mindsets make between space and time, which they locate on the same level, is in fact wrong. In the primitive mindset, as myths and rituals show us, space and time are one but it is time that is primary. Myth always has a historical form and it is in the sacred temples renewed by ritual that sacred places and objects are thought to be particularly worthy of veneration. The same is true for us. When living our lives, every place has a date and is felt as alive only inasmuch as that date occurs in the present moment and is made present as event. Only because of this can "the things" be felt as events and names become confused with verbs. Yet on the objective plane of consciousness, the relation is reversed because only space can be represented.

The event will always be found in the relation of two terms: The first is the *cuique* understood as the character of being grounded in existence [*esistenzialità*], and that is pointed out in the *hic et nunc*. The other is the spatial-temporal horizon from which the *èvenit* is thought to originate, and in which the *hic et nunc* is central. The first term is finite, the second infinite, and inasmuch as it is *ubique et semper*, it includes within it all of space and time. The divine is found here. This relation between finite and infinite is felt and not thought, and only as a felt relation is it real; the event can be understood only by seeing it against the background of what is experienced as existence. It is further on of every conscious thought. The first definition we have of this edge that the event makes present is ἄπειρον περιέχον [*apeiron periechon*]. Anaximander believed it to be divine and made it be the basis for the "governing of everything."

This last point is absolutely crucial. There are events and then there are events and each event has its own dimension and direction. All events, however, share the characteristics of the felt and lived presence of *apeiron periechon* [the indefinite nature of what surrounds the subject]. That which is proven by experience, by the phenomenology of religion, and by two of the most used systems for making sense of event: Stoicism, which marks the greatest closure [to event] and existentialism, in which the event appears most openly. In experience: Everyone knows that all events, in the moment in which we live them, contain—for an instant at least—everything there is of the eventful in the world [*tutto quanto v'è d'evento nel mondo*]. And the sensation that follows, in spatial order, is that of isolation and emptiness. With regard to the temporal order, a sort of break occurs in which time emerges and swirls. The one is inseparable from the other.

With regard to religion and its beginnings, we know that *mana* is seen, on one hand, as fixed and distinct. On the other, it is thought of as being so universal that the divine's unicity and its cosmic features were believed to be foreshadowed in the term *mana*. "Pantheists and monists," writes P. Saintyves, "are heirs to an immemorial tradition."[41] Now, this universality as lived universality is nothing other than the lived infinitude of the *periechon*. *Mana* tells us how every sacred site is experienced as the center of the world. At the same time, for primitive peoples the world has as its center a sacred site or object: tree, mountain, temple, and so forth. Accordingly, we see how each sacred time renews in itself the prototypical event in ritual, placed at the "origin," in a time beyond time (which at the same time encompasses it, the so-called time of myth). We also see how sacred time relates to the eternal. As has been frequently observed, the life of primitive peoples in fact takes place on the level of the cosmic and the eternal.

From the strictly structural analysis that I undertook in the course that I taught this year on the *Iliad*, I was able to confirm that while the representation in the poem occurs typically on one level and either ignores time or arranges it in linear fashion, on another level, just as soon as the action becomes tragic, an external space appears and the present forms a circle with the past and future. Typical in this regard is Book 22, through which we can account for theater. The scene does not come about because of some demand for realism, but because it is essential to the action, whatever the form through which action is represented; without it there is no drama. And as is the case for the *periechon*, where space and time together are one and include each other, so too must fate be understood in this way, which definitions, now obsolete, will see as constitutive of tragedy.

But *periechon* exists only in relation to *hic et nunc*: thus the three famous unities. My research into the poem revealed something else, while also supporting the relation I am talking about. It is a valuable principle: In the act in which a divinity is perceived as *praesens numen* [divine spirit], which is to say moves from form to power [*potenza*], everything is "divine." We can now explain what has been observed numerous times though no one has yet said why it was discovered. And that is, while the poet knows the divinity that every now and then intervenes in human affairs, for the hero that divinity is always the generic "divine" and is designated by the expressions, θεός θεοί [*theos theoi*], δαίμων [*daimon*]. Considering again Hermann Usener's theory with this principle in mind, we can say that the *Augenblicksgott* (the singular works better here than the plural) and the *Sondergötter* do not respond to two states of religious development but rather to two features of the same phenomenon.[42] The *deus certus* is only that when addressed in ritual and prayer. However, in the precise moment when he acts and is revealed as event, the god is always *numen* and is all that there is of the divine to be found in the world. This insight allows us to understand Roman religion in its entirety.

On the level of thought and philosophy then—just as for the Stoics where every *hic et nunc* is always concurrent with *ubique et semper*, so too for Heidegger's existentialism. The primary structure of *Dasein* is *Being-in-the-World*: a being in the world that is further on from that which we call consciousness and which is inseparable from the "comprehension" that *Dasein* enjoys over its *Sein*. *Dasein* is existence and the definition that Heidegger gives it cannot be understood apart from event. "Dasein is an entity," he writes (the pure *ti* of the Stoics, which is always *hic et nunc*), "which, in its very Being, comports itself towards that Being" (this is the fundamental sense of being that Antonio Rosmini speaks of and that Giovanni Gentile takes up in his *Philosophy of Art*).[43] He clarifies: "Furthermore, Dasein is an entity which in each case I myself am. Mineness belongs to any existent Dasein, and belongs to it as the condition which makes authenticity and inauthenticity possible" (being always my existence and as such cannot be represented). Jaspers's "Encompassing" [*das Umgreifende*] is analogous to Heidegger's *Being-in-the-World*, a concept through which Jaspers takes up Anaximander's *periechon*. Thus "Encompassing" is always lived and always infinite.

The relation between *hic et nunc* of the *cuique* and the *ubique et semper* of the *periechon* is dynamic and reciprocal. Thus we have the *Ineinander* with which Ernst Cassirer describes the space and time of the primitive mentality or, as he calls, of myth.[44] This makes Lévy-Bruhl's concept of participation intelligible and usable.[45] In *Ineinander* the figures become precarious, the substantiality of things is undone, everything is fluid, man perceives that the limits that he had come to trust about his own body now no longer hold, external space forces its way into the body, revealing and laying bare something in him that lies at the root of his breath, for which he does not have a word to describe it; it cannot be represented and it suspends him between the nothingness of the instant that falls and the nothingness of that which still has to burst forth. It makes a vortex out of duration in which the irreversibility of time is abolished.[46] Now everything is possible and thus on one side there is the *thambos*, the *horror*, the *Scheu* [dread] that Rudolf Otto speaks of, R. R. Marret's *awe* and on the other, *mana*, the *orenda*, the *numen tremendum*, God.[47]

Mankind's reaction to the breaking apart of time and the opening of space created by the event in and around him is to provide events with a structure and by enclosing them, normalize them. What distinguishes human civilization as well as individual lives is the different kinds of enclosure [*chiusura*] that the *periechon*'s space and time are given by them. The history of humanity (and the history of each one of us) is the history of these enclosures. Sacred moments, sacred sites, taboos, rituals and myths are nothing other than forms of enclosing. Our sense of a primitive civilization is given by the spatial-temporal picture in which the events are joined. And when anthropologists tell us that space and time of primitive peoples can always be qualified (which by the way is true for all of us), that qualification is constituted of nothing else but the position that in each part of space and for each division of time is given to events. All that cannot be arranged in such a context is marginalized, which will normally coincide with the territory that is inhabited, beyond which one finds the site of uncontrollable forces and often the dead. Thus the horror that the primitive experiences outside of his own territory and the horror for everything outside.

And here I come to your question. Are not all of these enclosures forms? And should one take precedence over the other? The response, it seems to me, is easy. If one takes a look at how both form and event begin, clearly event deserves more attention. If instead one considers function, remembering that life is possible in forms and thanks to forms, these forms not only are "essential" for the primitive world, but for ours as well, as they are generally for any culture on the grounds that it is only because of form that we are able to give a structure and a direction to that incommunicable thing that is the event. But—and this is the truly important point to remember—forms cannot be separated from events because the relation between forms and events is not about a *post* with respect to a *prius*. There is the same dynamic and reciprocal relation that we find between *hic et nunc* and the infinity of the *periechon*, which it reflects.

Let me try to make what I mean clearer by way of example. One of the most simple forms for enclosing an event is a name. We know how important names are in primitive worlds and for the sacred generally. The name, which spells out the power that is revealed in the event, supersedes the infinity that makes that power so frightening and limits it, allowing man to free himself from the *thambos* that paralyzes, and to direct his actions. Yet the very same name that gives form to event also allows the event to be reproduced and to make it present to us. That is why some names are *tabu*. The most obvious example of sacred enclosing that employs names are the *Indigitamenta*. If we think about myth, which is the most complex of the forms given to the event, the discussion remains the same. That myth is the figure of the event that works as an archetype for the ritual and in symbolic form explains the *dròmenon*.

There are rituals without being myths but a myth is not a myth without enjoying a relation to ritual and to the act of celebrating that ritual, in which only the myth can be lived as event. Separated from ritual, myth is downgraded to fable and so loses all connections with the sacred.

But your question implies another that really ought to be spelled out. It can be divided into three propositions: (1) What is the difference between the forms mentioned above and the form *kat' exochen*? (2) To what extent are the differences phenomenologically justified and then can the form *kat' exochen* be defended? (3) Can the form *kat' exochen* be thought of as a category and can one use the same name for the forms that are distinct from it, or do we have to find another?

In response to your first point, what I call "the form" par excellence is Plato and Aristotle's *eidos*. What defines it is the *autòtes*—that is, being for itself. Only *eidos* is καθ'αὐτό [*kath'hauto*]. What it is, is in itself and for itself, and excludes every relation. As such, it exhausts its essence in its capacity to be contemplated: That which is not capable of being contemplated in it is not. Instead the forms that man gives to the event have a completely different nature. None of them is καθ'αὐτό [*kath'hauto*] but instead are always κατ'ἄλλο τι [*kat'allo ti*] and ἕνεκά τινος ἄλλου [*heneka tinos allou*]. In addition, they cannot be understood apart from relationality. As forms they are capable of being contemplated but that capacity for being contemplated does not ever consume their essence; it is rather only a means for tapping into what is not visible in them and for seeing what they refer to, which excludes the capacity for being contemplated and can only be lived. They are symbols and functions but they are not *eide*, which is to say eventic forms [*forme eventiche*] and not "the forms." Thus they will always have a practical and not a theoretical value.

As for the second point, if phenomenology is, on the one hand, a verification of the phenomenon, and thus history, while on the other hand gives us a structural analysis of the phenomenon (and thus involves logic), that difference is justified both on the level of history and the level of logic; historically because such a sense of the form *kat' exochen* is found in many civilizations, but more or less only obscurely and incompletely. We find it quintessentially and more clearly (and in ways other civilizations never achieved) in Greek civilization. This explains its uniqueness, the fact that Greek civilization has at its heart such a sense of the form, which is manifested not only in their mode of reflection but above all in their thoughts on religion, art, and culture. It is logically justified because for us and our experience, which is the product of speculative thought across millennia, every proposition pivots either on essence or existence and essence and existence constitute the two sides within which logic moves. Yet essence is that which a thing is for itself and as such is, in traditional language, the form *kat' exochen* or the *eidos*. Furthermore, everything that is not pure essence in itself and for itself will always be the existence of someone in the act in which he or she lives it and verifies it, which then brings us back to the event. Given these two limits, if the event is a category, the other is the form as such.

Third point: should we keep one unique name or should we distinguish between them. I opt for one unique name because there are two extremes and all of the degrees in between happen thanks to the reduction in one or the increase in the other. The forms of event, understood as forms, enjoy the same right as does the form *kat' exochen* and at any moment they too can become forms *kat' exochen*, provided that the event to which they refer is voided and that these forms are only contemplated; as contemplated forms they are established absolutely. This is how the eventic forms of Mediterranean divinities became the solid forms of the Olympian gods. Similarly, the square was a symbol before Pythagoras and as such contained within it all of the qualities of the event. It was completely submerged in the world of magic. Observing this, Pythagoras saw the square as a square and nothing else and thus made it the basis of science.

This passage from the event to the eventic form and then to the form, *kat' exochén*, should not be taken so absolutely such that the three terms would become three distinct moments in a process that has only a single and unchangeable direction. Form and event are two categories and only as categories can they be distinguished. In our lived reality their relation is unstable, fluid, and always reversible. The same divinity that one moment appears as form, the next is perceived as event, and is taken mistakenly as the *periechon*. We do not live only an existence as the existentialists believe, nor only live as an essence, as Plato and Aristotle would have it. Instead we live an existence that is continually enclosed in essence and in an essence that in this very moment explodes into existence. This is why we always have to rely on our lived history. Nevertheless, the relation between form and event never stays the same. One of them inevitably wins and the degrees between form and event are infinite, allowing us to tell civilizations apart by their structure and to scale them. There are civilizations in which form dominates event and others in which event dominates form.

There is one thing to keep in mind though and that is that, the transition from one extreme to the other being qualitative, there is a limit beyond which the form, *kat' exochen,* stops and everything that follows has only a functional and symbolic value. At the same limit (and in the opposite sense), the event loses its cosmic qualities and is reduced to mere accident. The opposition between the two categories is not only logical. It is real and it makes life dramatic. The king cannot engage in dialectics with the court jester and vice versa. At the limit where form and event draw apart their respective kingdoms, there is death, be it of one of the two categories. Or it is man's death. It is here we find Plotinus's One, the Indian Brahma or Nothingness, or Lao Tze's Nothingness.

CARLO DIANO
July 1952

Phidias (c.490–430 B.C.)—Centaur and Lapith, from the Parthenon
frieze, Athens. Classical Greek, ca. 438–432 B.C. (South metope
XXVIII). © The Trustees of the British Museum / Art Resource, N.Y.

Dancing women. Sandstone metope from the Sanctuary of Hera at
Foce del Sele. Archaic Greek, ca. 570–560 B.C. Museo Archeologico
Nazionale, Paestum, Italy. © Vanni Archive / Art Resource, N.Y.

Kouros known as Apollo Milani. Marble statue. 6th century
B.C. Museo Archeologico, Florence, Italy. Photo: N. Grifoni.
© DeA Picture Library / Art Resource, N.Y.

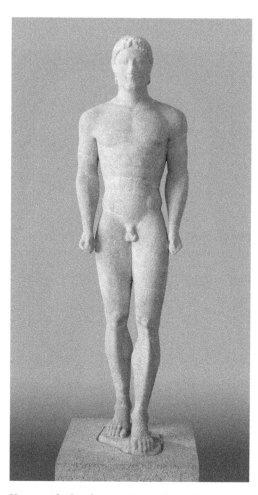

Kouros, idealized grave statue of a youth.
c. 540–530 B.C. Attica, Greece. Glyptothek,
Staatliche Antikensammlung, Munich, Germany.
© Vanni Archive / Art Resource, N.Y.

Apollo. Decoration of the Temple of Zeus in the Sanctuary
of Olympia. Parian marble. West pediment. 460 B.C.
Archaeological Museum of Olympia. Photo: Album / Art
Resource, N.Y.

Six youths in a palaestra (detail). Marble base of a Kouros statue with reliefs, attic. Originally the background of the relief was dark red. Marble, 79 × 29 cm. 510 B.C. National Archaeological Museum, Athens. Photo: Erich Lessing / Art Resource, N.Y.

Kore. Attic, 5th B.C. National Archaeological Museum,
Athens. Photo: Scala / Art Resource, N.Y.

Praxiteles (390–335 BC)—
Hermes and the infant Dionysus
(detail). 340–330 BC. Parian
marble. Discovered during
the excavations of the temple
of Hera in 1877 at Olympia.
Archaeological Museum of
Olympia, Greece. Photo:
Album / Art Resource, N.Y.

The Marathon Boy (detail of
head). Hellenistic, c. 330 B.C.
Bronze. Archaeological
Museum, Delphi, Greece.
Photo: Nimatallah / Art
Resource, N.Y.

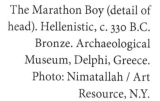

Apoxyomenos (The Scraper). Statue
representing an athlete scraping sweat and
dust from his body. Roman copy after an
original by Lysippos. Marble, 205 cm. Museo
Pio Clementino, Vatican Museums, Vatican
State. Photo: Universal Images Group / Art
Resource, N.Y.

Odysseus. Marble statuette. 2nd century A.D.
Imperial Roman copy of an early-to-mid 3rd century
B.C. Hellenistic original, from the Pergamon school.
Museo Archeologico, Venice, Italy. © Vanni Archive
/ Art Resource, N.Y.

NOTES

INTRODUCTION

1. Carlo Diano, *Forma ed evento. Principi per una interpretazione del mondo greco*, introduction by Remo Bodei (Venice: Marsilio Editori, 1994).

2. For the path of Heidegger's treatment of the event, see among others Hans Ruin, *Enigmatic Origins: Tracing the Theme of Historicity through Heidegger's Works* (Stockholm: Almqvist & Wiksell, 1994); Daniela Vallega-Neu, "*Ereignis*: The Event of Appropriation," in B. W. Davis, ed., *Martin Heidegger: Key Concepts* (Durham, N.C.: Acumen, 2010), 140–54, and especially the more extensive treatment in Daniela Vallega-Neu, *Heidegger's Poietic Writings: From* Contributions to Philosophy *to* The Event (Bloomington: Indiana University Press, 2018). See also Alain Badiou's treatment of the event in *Being and Event*, trans. Oliver Feltham (London: Continuum, 2005) and Alain Badiou, *Logics of Worlds: Being and Event II*, trans. Albert Toscano

(London: Continuum, 2009). A less technical account can be found in Alain Badiou, *Philosophy and the Event,* trans. Louise Burchill (Cambridge: Polity, 2013). For recent literary formalism, see Tom Eyers, *Speculative Formalism: Literature, Theory, and the Critical Present* (Evanston, Ill.: Northwestern University Press, 2017); Caroline Levine, *Forms. Whole, Rhythm, Hierarchy, Network* (Princeton: Princeton University Press, 2015); Anna Kornbluh, *The Order of Forms: Realism, Formalism, and Social Space* (Chicago: University of Chicago Press, 2019). On fact, event, and historicity, see for instance Bruno Latour, *We Have Never Been Modern* (Cambridge, Mass.: Harvard University Press, 1993), trans. Catherine Porter; and Mary Poovey's *A History of the Modern Fact: Problems of Knowledge in the Sciences of Wealth and Society* (Chicago: University of Chicago Press, 1998), and most recently Ethan Kleinberg, *Haunting History: For a Deconstructive Approach to the Past* (Stanford: Stanford University Press, 2017). See also Paul Ricoeur, "Le retour de l'Événement," *Mélanges de l'École française de Rome. Italie et Méditerranée* 104, no. 1 (1992): 29–35.

3. Jean Pierre Vernant and Pierre Vidal-Naquet. *Tragedy and Myth in Ancient Greece* (Sussex, U.K.: Harvester Press, 1981), trans. Janet Lloyd. See also *Simone Weil's The Iliad or Poem of Force: A Critical Edition,* ed. and trans. James P. Holoka (Bern, Switzerland: Peter Lang, 2006).

4. On the Frankfurt School's long history of Philo-hellenism, see Katie Fleming, "Odysseus and Enlight-enment: Horkheimer and Adorno's *Dialektik der Aufklärung,*" *International Journal of the Classical Tradition* 19, no. 2 (2012): 107–28.

5. "*Forma ed Evento* by Carlo Diano," review by J. Tate, *The Classical Review* (NS) 4, no. 3/4 (Dec. 1954): 295–96; here, 296.

6. For an overview of the philosophical and histori-cal context, see Enrico Berti, "La filosofia a Padova," *Rivista di Filosofia* 91, no. 2 (2000): 197–217.

7. Aristotle, *Physics, Volume 1: Books 1–4.* Translated by P. H. Wicksteed, F. M. Cornford. Loeb Classical Library 228 (Cambridge, Mass.: Harvard University Press, 1957), 157. See Jacques Lacan, "*Tyche* and *automa-ton,*" in Jacques Lacan, Jacques-Alain Miller, and Alan Sheridan, *The Four Fundamental Concepts of Psycho-Analysis* (London: Penguin, 1994). See also Mladen Dolar, "Tyche, clinamen, den," *Continental Philosophy Review* 46, no. 2: 223–39.

8. "O luce etterna che sola in te sidi / sola t'intendi, e da te intelletta / e intendente te ami e arridi!" (O Light Eterne, sole in thyself that dwellest, / Sole know-est thyself, and known unto thyself / And knowing, lovest and smilest on thyself), Dante Alighieri, *Parad-iso*, 33, 124–26, in *Divine Comedy*, trans. Henry Wad-sworth Longfellow (Boston: Fields, Osgood, & Co., 1871), 301.

9. Jan Łukasiewicz, *Aristotle's Syllogistic from the Standpoint of Modern Formal Logic*, second edition (Oxford: Clarendon Press, 1957). Łukasiewicz's 1950–57 arguments—which proved decisive to the establishment of modal logic as of the early 1960s—are adumbrated in his 1910 *O Zasadzie Sprzeczności u Arystotelesa. Studium Krytyczne* [*On the Principle of Contradiction in Aristotle. A Critical Study*] (Krakow: Polska Akademia Umiejętności). In English translation, "On the Principle of Contradiction in Aristotle," trans. V. Wedin, *Review of Metaphysics* 24 (1971): 485–509; and in Łukasiewicz, *O logice Stoików* (On the Logic of the Stoics), *Przeglad Filozoficzny* 30 (1927). The Italian translations of Łukasiewicz's work are in *La sillogistica di Aristotele*, trans. C. Negro; introduction by Czeslaw Lejewski (Brescia: Morcelliana, 1964) and *Del principio di con-traddizione in Aristotele*, ed. Gabriele Franci and Clau-dio Antonio Testi, introduction by Maurizio Matteuzzi (Macerata: Quodlibet, 2003). A very useful contempo-raneous account of the discovery and development of the Aristotelian-Stoic syllogism's differences is in I. M. Bochenski, *Ancient Formal Logic* (Amsterdam: North-Holland Publishing Company, 1951).

10. *Princeton Readings in Political Thought: Essen-tial Texts from Plato to Populism*, ed. Mitchell Cohen (Princeton, Princeton University Press, 2018), 540–42.

11. The history of the essay in the *Enciclopedia Itali-ana* is well enough known. Signed by Mussolini, it con-sists of a section written and previously published by

Gentile, in Giovanni Gentile, *Origini e Dottrina del Fascismo* (Rome: Libreria Del Littorio, 1929), and sections attributable directly to Mussolini. Alongside its publication in the *Enciclopedia,* the article appeared as Benito Mussolini, *La dottrina del Fascismo. Con una storia del movimento fascista di Gioacchino Volpe* (Milano: Treves-Treccani-Tumminelli, 1932). Eric Voegelin, *The Authoritarian State* (1936), focuses on just this expression, *anima dell'anima,* to mark the "astonishing coincidence between the German and the Italian theoretical versions" of "the relationship between the individual and the supraindividual community that can be applied to every concrete community," and not only to the Fascist and National Socialist States. Voegelin is analyzing the Mussolini-Gentile passage I cite, alongside Ernst Rudolf Huber, "Die Totalität des völkischen Staates," *Die Tat* 36, no. 1 (1934): 30–42. See Eric Voegelin, *The Authoritarian State, Collected Works of Eric Voegelin,* vol. 4., ed. Gilbert Weiss, trans. Ruth Hein (Columbia: University of Missouri Press, 1999), 73–74.

12. Lucretius, *On the Nature of Things,* tr. Martin Ferguson Smith (Indianapolis: Hackett, 2001), 75. "Nihil animale sine sensu, nihil sensuale sine anima, et ur impressius dixerim animae anima sensus est," Tertullian, *De carne christi* 44; Giordano Bruno, *The Expulsion of the Triumphant Beast,* 240; see also Bruno, "La divinità, che è come l'anima dell'anima, la quale è tutta in tutto," *De l'infinito,* Utet, 55; BL, 103.

1. [All endnotes—including citations, references, and commentary—are contributed by the translators.] "For no one deliberates about the past, but about what is future and capable of being otherwise, while what is past is not capable of not having taken place; hence Agathon is right in saying: For this alone is lacking even to God, To make undone things that have once been done" (4:2). Aristotle, *Nicomachean Ethics*, trans. W. D. Ross, accessed December 10, 2016, http://classics .mit.edu/Aristotle/nicomachaen.mb.txt.

2. Aristotle, *Metaphysics*, trans. W. D. Ross, accessed December 10, 2016, http://classics.mit.edu/Aristotle/ metaphysics.mb.txt.

3. See A. A. Long and D. N. Medley, eds., *The Helle-nistic Philosophers*, vol. 1 (New York: Cambridge University Press, 1987), 304.

4. "The foregoing argument, then, has served to clear up the point about which we raised a difficulty at the outset—why is it that instead of all things being either in motion or at rest, or some things being always in motion and the remainder always at rest, there are things that are sometimes in motion and sometimes not? The cause of this is now plain: it is because, while some things are moved by an eternal unmoved movent and are therefore always in motion, other things are moved by a movent that is in motion and changing, so that they too must change. But the unmoved movent,

as has been said, since it remains permanently simple and unvarying and in the same state, will cause motion that is one and simple." Aristotle, *Physics*, trans. R. P. Hardie and R. K. Gaye, accessed December 10, 2016, http://classics.mit.edu/Aristotle/physics.mb.txt.

5. "O luce etterna che sola in te sidi / sola t'intendi, e da te intelletta / e intendente te ami e arridi!" ("O Light Eterne, sole in thyself that dwellest, / Sole knowest thyself, and known unto thyself / And knowing, lovest and smilest on thyself"), Dante Alighieri, *Paradiso*, 33, 124–26, in *Divine Comedy*, trans. Henry Wadsworth Longfellow (Boston: Fields, Osgood, & Co., 1871), 301.

6. See Long and Medley, eds., *The Hellenistic Philosophers*, vol. 1, 276.

7. On *heimarmene* (the spun thread of destiny), see Frederick Ahl, *Two Faces of Oedipus:* Sophocles' Oedipus Tyrannus *and Seneca's* Oedipus (Ithaca: Cornell University Press, 2008), 26–27.

8. Aratus, *Phaenomena*, trans. G. R. Mair, accessed December 20, 2016, http://www.theoi.com/Text/Aratus Phaenomena.html.

9. Cicero, *On Fate*, accessed November 3, 2016, http://www.informationphilosopher.com/solutions/ philosophers/cicero/de_fato_english.html.

10. Long and Medley, eds., *The Hellenistic Philosophers*, vol. 1, 23.

11. Giuseppe Furlani, "Sul concetto del destino nella religione babilonese e assira," *Aegyptus* 9, no. 304 (December 1928), 223.

12. Max Pohlenz, *Die Stoa: Geschichte einer geistigen Bewegung* (Göttingen: Vandenhoeck & Ruprecht, 1992). See too Edwyn Bevan, *Stoics and Sophists* (Oxford: Clarendon Press, 1913).

13. *Tragicorum Graecorum Fragmenta*, vol. 5: *Euripides*, ed. Richard Kann (Gottingen: Vandenhoeck & Ruprecht, 2007), 820b, 4f.

14. Aristotle, *Physics*, 196b 7–9. See too W. K. C. Guthrie, *A History of Greek Philosophy*, vol. 6 (Cambridge: Cambridge University Press, 1981), 236–37.

15. See Jon D. Mikalson, *Religion in Hellenistic Athens* (Berkeley: University of California Press, 1998), 62–64.

16. *The Teubner Anthologia Lyrica Graeca*, ed. E. Diehl, vol. 1 (Leipzig: Teubner, 1936), 640.

17. *The Works of Horace: English Notes, Critical and Explanatory*, ed. Charles Anthon (New York: Harper & Brothers, 1849), 78.

18. Gerard van der Leeuw, *Religion in Essence and Manifestation* (Princeton: Princeton University Press, 2014), 25.

19. "How be it, if fortune be opposite, nothing may prosper a man, nor may the fatal disposition of the divine providence be avoided or changed by wise counsel, nor by any wholesome remedy" (Apuleius, *The Golden Ass: Being the Metamorphoses of Lucius* Apuleius, trans. W. Aldington [New York: G. P. Putnam's Sons, 1922], 401).

20. Cleanthes, "The Hymn to Zeus by Cleanthes," accessed November 11, 2016, https://philosophy-of-cbt .com/2012/11/08/the-hymn-to-zeus-by-cleanthes/.

21. Horace, *Satires. Epistles. The Art of Poetry*, trans. H. Rushton Fairclough (Cambridge, Mass.: Harvard University Press, 1926), 362–63. The full cite is: "The one will not wait for a purple mantle; he will put on anything and walk through the most crowded streets, and in no inelegant fashion will play either part. The other will shun a cloak woven at Miletus as worse than a dog or a snake, and will die of cold if you do not give him back his rags. Give them back and let him live his uncouth life."

22. Seneca, *Epistles*, accessed December 20, 2016, http://www.stoics.com/seneca_epistles_book_1.html #'XXXIV1.

23. Plato, *Republic*, accessed December 21, 2016, http://classics.mit.edu/Plato/republic.8.vii.html.

24. "Further, there cannot be a special sense-organ for the common sensibles either, [15] i.e. the objects which we perceive incidentally through this or that special sense, e.g. movement, rest, figure, magnitude, number, unity; for all these we perceive by movement, e.g. magnitude by movement, and therefore also figure (for figure is a species of magnitude), what is at rest by the absence of movement: number is perceived by the negation of continuity, and by the special sensibles; for each sense [20] perceives one class of sensible objects."

Aristotle, "On the Soul," 425a13, in *The Complete Works of Aristotle: The Revised Oxford Translation*, 2 vols., ed. Jonathan Barnes (Princeton: Princeton University Press, 1984), 1:1163.

25. Aristotle, *Metaphysics*, 1034a5–8 (7:8).

26. "Now practical wisdom is concerned with action; therefore one should have both forms of it, or the latter in preference to the former. Here, too, there must be a controlling kind" (Aristotle, *Nicomachean Ethics*, Book 6:7, 4387, in *The Collected Works of Aristotle*).

27. *The Odes of Pindar*, trans. Richard Lattimore (Chicago: The University of Chicago Press Chicago: 1947), accessed December 21, 2016, https://archive.org/stream/odesofpindaro35276mbp/odesofpindaro35276mbp_djvu.txt.

28. Walter F. Otto, *The Homeric Gods*, trans. Moses Hadas (New York: Pantheon, 1954).

29. On mystery cults, goddesses, and mothers, see Walter Burkett, *Greek Religion: Archaic and Classical* (Cambridge, Mass.: Harvard University Press), 1987.

30. See Aristotle, *Physics*, Book 6:4–5.

31. Homer, *The Odyssey*, trans. Robert Fagles (New York: Penguin Putnam, 1996), 46–50.

32. Diano refers here to Book 24 of the *Iliad*, in which Hector's dead body is redeemed by Priam.

33. Homer, *The Iliad*, trans. Robert Fagles (New York: Penguin Putnam, 1990), 113; 120.

34. Homer, *Odyssey*, 9:16.

35. Homer, *Odyssey*, 9:14.

36. Homer, *Iliad*, 299.

37. "Many and marvellous the things of fear / Earth's breast doth bear; / And the sea's lap with many monsters teems, / And windy levin-bolts and meteor gleams / Breed many deadly things-Unknown and flying forms, with fear upon their wings, / And in their tread is death; / And rushing whirlwinds, of whose blasting breath / Man's tongue can tell. / But who can tell aright the fiercer thing, The aweless soul, within man's breast inhabiting?" Aeschylus, *Choephori*, accessed December 22, 2016, http://classics.mit.edu/Aeschylus/choephori.html.

38. Homer, *Iliad*, 262.

39. Pietro de Francisci, *Giornale Critico della Filosofia Italiana* (July–September, 1953): 69. For the details of Francisci's letter and Diano's response, see Francesco Verde's helpful "Forma e storia, evento e natura: Carlo Diano," accessed December 22, 2016, http://www.syze tesis.it/documenti/archivio/anno3/f1/9%20articolo%20 Verde_2016_1.pdf.

40. Verde believes that on this score Diano has in mind fragment 125 of *Incertae fabulae*. See R. Kassel and C. Austin, *Poeta Comici Graeci*, 6:2 (Berolini: Novi Eboraci: W. de Gruyter, 1983), S. 400, Nr. 125.

41. Pierre Saintyves, *La force magique* (Paris: E. Nourry, 1914), 46; cited in G. Van der Leeuw, *Phäenomenologie der Religion* (Tübingen: Mohr Siebeck, 1956), 16.

42. Hermann Usener, *Götternamen: Versuch einer Lehre von der Religiösen Begriffsbildung* (Bonn: Verlag von Friedrich Cohen, 1896), 75–76.

43. Martin Heidegger, *Being and Time*, trans. John Macquarrie and Edward Robinson (Oxford: Blackwell, 1962), 78.

44. Ernst Cassirer, *The Philosophy of Symbolic Forms, Volume 2: Mythical Thought*, trans. Ralph Manheim (New Haven: Yale University Press, 1955), esp. 147–50.

45. Lucien Lévy-Bruhl, *Primitive Mentality* (London: Allen & Unwin, 1923).

46. See on this Van der Leeuw, *La religion*, 379.

47. On Rudolf Otto's notion of *Scheu*, see his *The Idea of the Holy*, trans. John W. Harvey (Oxford: Oxford University Press, 1923). For Marret and awe, see *The Threshold of Religion* (London: Methuen & Co., 1909).

CONTRIBUTORS

Carlo Alberto Diano (1902–1974) was one of the most important Hellenists and philologists of the twentieth century. In addition to his numerous translations, he is also the author of *Linee per una fenomenologia dell'arte*.

Jacques Lezra is professor and chair of Hispanic studies at the University of California, Riverside. His books include *Untranslating Machines: A Genealogy for the Ends of Global Thought*; *Wild Materialism: The Ethic of Terror and the Modern Republic* (translated into Spanish and Chinese); and *Unspeakable Subjects: The Genealogy of the Event in Early Modern Europe*. With Emily Apter and Michael Wood, he is the coeditor of Barbara Cassin's *Dictionary of Untranslatables*.

Timothy C. Campbell is professor of Italian at Cornell University. In addition to his translations of Roberto Esposito's *Bios: Biopolitics and Philosophy and Communitas: The Origin and Destiny of Community*, he is most recently the author of *The Techne of Giving: Cinema and the Generous Form of Life* (2017) from Fordham University Press.

Lia Turtas recently received her PhD in Romance studies at Cornell University. Her current research centers on reading the figure of automatism across key moments of Italian cinema by drawing upon posthumanism, film theory, and Italian thought.

COMMONALITIES

Timothy C. Campbell, series editor

Roberto Esposito, *Terms of the Political: Community, Immunity, Biopolitics*. Translated by Rhiannon Noel Welch. Introduction by Vanessa Lemm.

Maurizio Ferraris, *Documentality: Why It Is Necessary to Leave Traces*. Translated by Richard Davies.

Dimitris Vardoulakis, *Sovereignty and Its Other: Toward the Dejustification of Violence*.

Anne Emmanuelle Berger, *The Queer Turn in Feminism: Identities, Sexualities, and the Theater of Gender*. Translated by Catherine Porter.

James D. Lilley, *Common Things: Romance and the Aesthetics of Belonging in Atlantic Modernity*.

Jean-Luc Nancy, *Identity: Fragments, Frankness*. Translated by François Raffoul.

Miguel Vatter, *Between Form and Event: Machiavelli's Theory of Political Freedom.*

Miguel Vatter, *The Republic of the Living: Biopolitics and the Critique of Civil Society.*

Maurizio Ferraris, *Where Are You? An Ontology of the Cell Phone.* Translated by Sarah De Sanctis.

Irving Goh, *The Reject: Community, Politics, and Religion after the Subject.*

Kevin Attell, *Giorgio Agamben: Beyond the Threshold of Deconstruction.*

J. Hillis Miller, *Communities in Fiction.*

Remo Bodei, *The Life of Things, the Love of Things.* Translated by Murtha Baca.

Gabriela Basterra, *The Subject of Freedom: Kant, Levinas.*

Roberto Esposito, *Categories of the Impolitical.* Translated by Connal Parsley.

Roberto Esposito, *Two: The Machine of Political Theology and the Place of Thought.* Translated by Zakiya Hanafi.

Akiba Lerner, *Redemptive Hope: From the Age of Enlightenment to the Age of Obama.*

Adriana Cavarero and Angelo Scola, *Thou Shalt Not Kill: A Political and Theological Dialogue*. Translated by Margaret Adams Groesbeck and Adam Sitze.

Massimo Cacciari, *Europe and Empire: On the Political Forms of Globalization*. Edited by Alessandro Carrera, Translated by Massimo Verdicchio.

Emanuele Coccia, *Sensible Life: A Micro-ontology of the Image*. Translated by Scott Stuart, Introduction by Kevin Attell.

Timothy C. Campbell, *The Techne of Giving: Cinema and the Generous Forms of Life*.

Étienne Balibar, *Citizen Subject: Foundations for Philosophical Anthropology*. Translated by Steven Miller, Foreword by Emily Apter.

Ashon T. Crawley, *Blackpentecostal Breath: The Aesthetics of Possibility*.

Terrion L. Williamson, *Scandalize My Name: Black Feminist Practice and the Making of Black Social Life*.

Jean-Luc Nancy, *The Disavowed Community*. Translated by Philip Armstrong.

Roberto Esposito, *The Origin of the Political: Hannah Arendt or Simone Weil?* Translated by Vincenzo Binetti and Gareth Williams.

Dimitris Vardoulakis, *Stasis before the State:*
Nine Theses on Agonistic Democracy.

Nicholas Heron, *Liturgical Power: Between Economic*
and Political Theology.

Emanuele Coccia, *Goods: Advertising, Urban Space,*
and the Moral Law of the Image. Translated
by Marissa Gemma.

James Edward Ford III, *Thinking Through Crisis:*
Depression-Era Black Literature, Theory, and Politics.

Étienne Balibar, *On Universals: Constructing and*
Deconstructing Community. Translated by Joshua
David Jordan.

Lightning Source UK Ltd.
Milton Keynes UK
UKHW042354070620
364476UK00016BA/415